CAMBRIDGE MUSIC HANDBOOKS

Liszt: Sonata in B Minor

CAMBRIDGE MUSIC HANDBOOKS

GENERAL EDITOR Julian Rushton

Cambridge Music Handbooks provide accessible introductions to major musical works.

Published titles

Liszt: Sonata in B Minor

Kenneth Hamilton

Published by the Press Syndicate of the University of Cambridge
The Pitt Building, Trumpington Street, Cambridge CB2 1RP
40 West 20th Street, New York, NY 10011–4211, USA
10 Stamford Road, Oakleigh, Melbourne 3166, Australia

© Cambridge University Press 1996

First published 1996

Printed in Great Britain at the University Press, Cambridge

A catalogue record for this book is available from the British Library

Library of Congress cataloguing in publication data
Hamilton, Kenneth, 1963–
Liszt, Sonata in B Minor / Kenneth Hamilton.
p. cm. – (Cambridge music handbooks)
Includes bibliographical references (p.) and index.
ISBN 0 521 46570 2 (hardback) – ISBN 0 521 46963 5 (paperback)
1. Liszt, Franz, 1811–1886. Sonata, piano, B minor.
I. Title. II. Series.
ML410.L7H258 1996
786.2' 183 – dc20 95-49839 CIP MN

ISBN 0 521 46570 2 hardback
ISBN 0 521 46963 5 paperback

AH

For my piano teachers Alexa Maxwell and Ronald Stevenson;
and in memory of Lawrence Glover, with whom
I first studied the Liszt Sonata.

Contents

Preface

Were all Liszt's works, with the exception of the Sonata in B minor, to be engulfed in flames like the books of the ancient library of Alexandria, the Sonata would still be enough to rank him as one of the greatest Romantic composers. That this statement can now seem unexceptionable would have astonished many of Liszt's contemporaries, who were confident that he was merely a virtuoso pianist suffering from delusions of compositional talent. Most astonished of all would have been Eduard Hanslick, the grotesquely influential Viennese critic, and patron saint of those who sit in judgement on that which they are unable to do themselves. After hearing Liszt's pupil Hans von Bülow perform the Sonata in Vienna in 1881, Dr Hanslick's diagnosis left little ground for hope: 'Anyone who has heard this and finds it beautiful is beyond help.'[1] Liszt had by this time become inured to such criticisms, and adopted an attitude of stoic silence. He nevertheless took solace in the enthusiasm of his pupils. On discovering that Arthur Friedheim had memorised not just the solo part, but the entire orchestral accompaniment of his Piano Concerto in A, Liszt turned to face his assembled students and declared 'I can wait!' His wait has been long, and the greater part of it posthumous, but now, at the end of the twentieth century, his music is as much part of the central repertoire as that of Chopin or Brahms. The Sonata itself boasts – almost unbelievably – more than fifty currently available recordings, a plethora of editions, a published manuscript facsimile and perhaps even over-exposure in the concert hall. Few young pianists with pretentions to virtuosity can have avoided hours of lonely toil over the celebrated octave passages, or over the creation of the requisite pensive atmosphere at the beginning of the piece. My own fascination with the Sonata dates from learning it as a teenaged piano student. Since then I have performed it in public dozens of times and, I hope, my interpretation has matured somewhat, yet increased familiarity has only underlined the infinite variety of this remarkable music.

This variety is reflected in the academic literature on the Sonata, which is

more extensive than that of any other work by Liszt, the *Faust* Symphony
included, a fact easily verified by a perusal of Michael Saffle's highly useful
Franz Liszt: A Guide to Research (New York, 1991). The oldest of these studies
to retain some influence is Paul Egert's *Die Klaviersonate in H-moll von Franz
Liszt* (for details of this, and other works mentioned below, see the Select
bibliography). Egert is the source of the view that the Sonata is based on one
single theme (the initial descending scale) that we find reiterated by Claudio
Arrau in 'Some Final Thoughts' in the Henle edition of the manuscript
facsimile. The opinion of a musician as outstanding as Arrau commands
respect, but I find Egert's arguments forced and unconvincing. Most
subsequent writers also forsook Egert's quest for the chimera of thematic
unity, in particular W. S. Newman, R. M. Longyear and S. Winklhofer, who
have undoubtedly contributed the most significant detailed analyses of the
Sonata. Their work will be discussed later in this Handbook. To follow this
discussion the general reader will need one of the several reliable editions of
the Sonata available today. (The original edition, by Breitkopf und Härtel
(1854), can now only be found in larger libraries.) My references to bar
numbers follow those in the New Liszt Edition (Editio Musica Budapest). The
'Old Liszt Edition', as that produced under the editorship of the *Franz-Liszt-
Stiftung* is often known, is now obtainable in an excellent Dover reprint. The
editor was Liszt's pupil José Vianna da Motta, and his preface reproduces
several deleted passages from the Sonata autograph, in addition to the original
coda. Other Liszt pupils to edit the Sonata include Rosenthal, Joseffy,
D'Albert and Sauer. Sauer's Peters edition gives two additions to the text
marked as 'according to Liszt's intentions'. These will be commented upon
later, as will the instructions for performance contained in Ramann's *Liszt
Pädagogium*, derived from notes taken by Liszt's student August Stradal. The
recent reprint of the *Pädagogium* contains a valuable preface by Alfred
Brendel, one of the finest interpreters of the Sonata. Brendel's own analysis
of the piece, contained in *Music Sounded Out*, is a model of good sense.

Of especial interest is the Henle facsimile edition of the Sonata manuscript,
published in 1973. Handsome as this is, it does have one major flaw. Any
revisions later pasted over using collettes (additional pieces of manuscript
paper) conceal the unrevised text underneath. Fortunately Winklhofer has
transcribed passages underneath collettes, and indeed also those found on the
reverse of the collettes themselves, in her book, which must be used in
conjunction with the facsimile for a full understanding of the manuscript's
compositional process. The accuracy of the colour reproduction in the
facsimile has occasioned some pedantic carping, but this seems a minor issue

indeed considering the value of the publication as a whole. Few documents give a more immediate insight into Liszt's feverish creativity during his Weimar years, and musicians would be well advised to seek out a library copy. Unfortunately the facsimile's price puts it out of the reach of casual readers unless, like Wagner, they make most of their purchases with other people's money.

Acknowledgements

I should like to thank Ian Ledsham and the staff of Birmingham University Music Library for their speed and patience in dealing with my various bibliographical requests. Birmingham University Music Department was generous in releasing me from certain tedious commitments in order to facilitate writing up, and Sue Weldon saved me from the consequences of my technological ineptitude by agreeing to word-process the manuscript. Duncan Fielden kindly found time to set up the music examples in the breaks between Dr Who episodes. Julian Rushton made several perceptive comments on the initial version of the book, and saved me from a career-destroying misquote from Handel's little-known oratorio *Messiah*. Leslie Howard, whose scholarship is no less impressive than his pianism, corrected various errors in the final manuscript. Needless to say, had it not been for the notorious impatience and relentless nagging of Penny Souster at Cambridge University Press, this book would never have been finished at all.

1

Introduction

Perhaps the greatest source of wonder in Liszt's life was that he composed anything at all, let alone anything of lasting greatness. The man who, from an early age, had crisscrossed Europe as the greatest travelling virtuoso, providing, with the onset of puberty, much material for gossip columns, might have been forgiven for taking the Wildean view, 'My art is my life', and leaving it at that. Even after he settled down in Weimar in 1848, to devote himself to composition, his existence was scarcely less hectic, and the B minor Sonata, 'finished 2nd February 1853' according to Liszt's manuscript note, was merely one of a maelstrom of activities. Although he had made at least two preliminary sketches of themes for the Sonata[1] – one of the opening two motifs in 1851, another of the beginning of the Andante sostenuto in 1849 – it is likely that the main compositional work was started in the latter part of 1852.

Exactly how Liszt could have found the time to compose is difficult to imagine. In June 1852 he had conducted two concerts at the Ballenstedt-am-Harz music festival, the programmes including Beethoven's Ninth Symphony and Berlioz's *Harold in Italy*. In September he conducted Verdi's *Ernani*. A Berlioz week in Weimar was scheduled for November, when the *Romeo and Juliet* Symphony, the *Damnation of Faust* and *Benvenuto Cellini* were performed. Looming on the horizon after this was a Wagner festival for February 1853, by which time *The Flying Dutchman*, *Tannhäuser* and *Lohengrin* had to be fully rehearsed. If this immersion in some of the most difficult avant-garde music were not enough, Liszt's private life was also running less than smoothly. His mother had visited Weimar in the summer of 1852 and had promptly broken her ankle, an injury requiring several months convalescence at the Altenberg, the house Liszt shared with his mistress, Princess Carolyne zu Sayn-Wittgenstein. In September the Princess's estranged husband Nicholas arrived to discuss divorce proceedings – an event Liszt might have wished had taken place in his mother's absence. It is not surprising that by 16 February 1853, only two weeks after the completion of the Sonata, he was at the end of his tether, writing a letter to Duke Carl

Alexander deploring musical conditions in Weimar, and giving every impression that he was on the brink of resigning from his post as Kapellmeister.

Fortunately, Liszt thought better of leaving Weimar; otherwise the most musically productive period of his life would have been cut short. The astonishing fact remains that during the very months when it is difficult to see how he found time to concentrate on the Sonata, he also composed the *Hungarian* Fantasy for piano and orchestra and continued work on several other pieces. Perhaps his enthusiastic consumption of cheap cigars and cognac helped him along. At any rate, by mid-1854 he had written to his friend Louis Köhler:

For the present I allow myself to send you my Sonata, which has just been published at Härtel's. You will soon receive another long piece, *Scherzo and March*, and in the course of the summer my *Years of Pilgrimage Suite of Piano Compositions* will appear at Schott's; two years – Switzerland and Italy. With these pieces I shall have done for the present with the piano, in order to devote myself exclusively to orchestral compositions, and to attempt more in that domain which has for a long time become an inner necessity. Seven of the symphonic poems are perfectly ready and written out.[2]

In fact, the Italian volume of *Years of Pilgrimage* was not published until 1858. *Switzerland* came out in 1855, but the first six (not seven) symphonic poems were held up until 1856. Undoubtedly Liszt's habit of constant revision caused the delay in their appearance. More importantly, the letter shows that he regarded the Sonata, and the associated pieces, as the zenith of his work as a composer for the piano.

The Sonata was not only a challenge to those who regarded Liszt as merely a performer, but also a culmination of a long period of thought on the direction of contemporary music. Those interested in the genesis of Romantic music are lucky that composers such as Berlioz, Liszt, Schumann and Wagner were verbally, as well as musically, articulate. By following Liszt's correspondence, both public and private, it is fairly easy to chart what he regarded as discrete stages of his career. When the most brilliant of his virtuoso successes were yet ahead, the idea of being 'done for the present with the piano' was inconceivable to him. A letter to Adolphe Pictet, written for general consumption and published in the *Revue et gazette musicale* on 11 February 1838, states as much in florid prose:

... even you are surprised to see me so exclusively occupied with the piano, and so little hurried to assay the wider field of symphonic and dramatic composition ... You do not know that to talk to me about giving up the piano is to make me look upon a day of sorrow ... For, you see, my piano is to me as his ship is to a sailor, or his steed to an Arab, even more perhaps, for until now my piano is me, it is my speech – my life. It is the intimate repository of all that went on in my mind during the most passionate days of my youth ... and you, my friend, would like me to abandon it to run after the more glittering successes of the theatre and the orchestra? Oh, no! Even if I admitted that which you too easily assert, that I am now ready for music of this kind, my firm resolution is not to abandon the study and development of the piano until I have accomplished everything possible with it.[3]

One might have been forgiven for thinking that by the end of 1838 Liszt had already scaled the Himalayas of piano virtuosity. The previous year he had completed the *Douze grandes études*, soon to be followed by the six *Etudes d'après Paganini* (or rather seven, for one appeared in two versions). The *Paganini Studies* sported a dedication to Clara Schumann, although Liszt must have realised that she would be scarcely capable of playing them even if she had wanted to – and that was unlikely given her abomination of most of his music. Taken together, the two sets of studies confirmed Liszt as the pre-eminent piano technician of his era, a fact admitted even by those who preferred the playing of his nearest rival, Sigismond Thalberg. (The *Douze grandes études* were further revised in 1851 to become *Douze études d'exécution transcendante*. A final version of the *Paganini Studies* was made around the same time.) How far Liszt had progressed can be seen by a comparison of the *Douze grandes études* with their original source, the *études en douze exercices* published by the teenaged composer in 1826. The 1826 studies, though musically negligible, are a fair compendium of early nineteenth-century piano technique – a technique based on brilliant passage work, almost all of which can be accomplished by finger-action alone, with relatively little required of the wrist other than it remain steady and relaxed. This, of course, was typical harpsichord technique, and was easily transferred to the early piano with its light touch and shallow fall of key. Isolated finger-action was so prized that various mechanical devices were sometimes fitted to the piano in order to ensure that the student was unable to use wrist-action. Ludicrous as these might seem now, such contraptions were recommended by pre-eminent pianists such as Kalkbrenner, and even by the young Liszt, although there is no evidence that he himself ever used one. (He did, however, have a practice piano made with a specially heavy action.)

The doctrine of playing with a quiet wrist lasted, in some cases, well into the twentieth century. Many aging pianists reminisce of being forced by their teachers to play with coins lying on the back of the hands. Should a coin fall, then too much wrist-action was the culprit, a fault punished by a rap with a ruler across the offending joint. Of course, even by 1818, the date of the completion of Beethoven's *Hammerklavier* Sonata, op. 106, a freer piano technique was required, and it is no coincidence that Liszt was the first pianist to give a public performance of op. 106 nearly twenty years later. In doing so he had, according to Berlioz, accomplished a feat hitherto thought impossible. For pianists confined to the older style of piano technique, the octaves, chords and leaps of Liszt's later studies presented insurmountable difficulties. Inspired by Paganini's virtuosity on the violin and no doubt by the mould-breaking genius of his friend Chopin, Liszt had remodelled his technique in the early 1830s. The fantasy on Auber's *La fiancée* of 1829 had already shown him to be a consummate master of finger-dexterity. By the end of the next decade he had revolutionised his approach to piano sonority.

This achievement was not without its drawbacks for Liszt the composer. In the first place, most of his piano music was too difficult for other pianists to tackle, so public performance was limited to his own, admittedly frequent, concerts. In the second place, the thicket of technical hazards presented by works like the *Grandes études* distracted attention from their musical value. In his review of the studies for the *Neue Zeitschrift für Musik*, Schumann explicitly stated that Liszt's concentration on virtuosity had been at the expense of his development as a composer, an opinion that persists in some circles to this day. The fact that certain features of Liszt's harmonic style were as avant garde as his piano writing, was to his detractors yet another reason for accusing him of creative poverty. Had his musical language been as pedestrian as that of Herz or Pixis it would certainly have gained more immediate acceptance. One can sympathise to some extent with any musician of 1840 who put Liszt's studies on his piano stand, stared in bafflement at the jungle of seemingly impossible figurations, and decided to practise Thalberg's fantasy on Rossini's *Moses* instead. In their 1837 version, some of the studies are so texturally overloaded that they can sound jumbled even when well played, in particular the first two pages of the F minor study, which ironically is one of the best works in the set. With the later Weimar revision, its musical value is more apparent. Given the difficulties of the piano writing, it is not surprising that no one noticed that the F minor study and two others were innovative sonata forms strongly influenced by Beethoven, for these were composed at a time when the understanding of Beethoven shown by Liszt's fellow virtuosi was limited to putting a few chromatic runs under the slow-movement theme from the Seventh Symphony, and calling the resultant desecration *Souvenir de Beethoven*. In the years following the composition of his *Grandes études*, Liszt toured Europe as the greatest, and most highly paid virtuoso in the world. The latter accolade later passed to Anton Rubinstein and then to Paderewski. (Paderewski's level of fees was finally eclipsed in 1950s America by the singer Perry Como, a painful reminder to pianists of their decline in public esteem.)

Most of Liszt's compositional activity in the early 1840s was connected to his concert tours, manifested in a large number of fantasies and transcriptions of operatic melodies. The best of these works, like the fantasies on Meyerbeer's *Robert le Diable* or Mozart's *Don Giovanni*, are in effect original works offering a striking new perspective on the operas' themes. They also represent the further honing and refining of Liszt's keyboard style, and were regarded by figures as diverse as Brahms and Busoni as a pinnacle of virtuoso technique.

These early years of the 1840s are usually considered as the height of Liszt's *Glanzperiode* – his 'glory days' as a touring virtuoso. In 1842 he accepted a position as honorary Kapellmeister in Weimar, though the concert tours continued until 1848, when he took up permanent residence in the town. Whilst Liszt's pianistic endeavours met with unparalleled success all over Europe, the tours were not without their difficult moments, which included the occasional near-empty hall, and an unexpected trip in an open cattle wagon during a visit to Scotland. Such incidents no doubt encouraged humility in the 'King of pianists', who otherwise was taxed only with the admiration of the adoring masses. It would have been easy for Liszt to ride on his success and keep only a few bravura works in his repertoire, routinely to be trotted out at each new venue. Such tactics are not unknown today. Liszt, however, was gifted – or afflicted – with an intellectual restlessness that prompted him to explore a wide range of music. A catalogue of his concert repertoire that he had made soon after settling in Weimar includes not only a vast array of crowd-pleasers, but also sonatas by Beethoven, Hummel, Weber and Schumann – hardly standard concert-fare for the period.

As the 1840s progressed, Liszt's thoughts turned to the establishment of his reputation as a composer. The 'glittering successes of the theatre and the orchestra' that he had turned his back on in favour of the piano now beckoned with inviting allure. Though he cherished some hopes of eventually succeeding Donizetti as Kapellmeister in Vienna, his position as Kapellmeister at Weimar lay in readiness for whenever he should decide finally to give up his gypsy life. The catalyst was the meeting in Kiev in 1847 with Princess Carolyne zu Sayn-Wittgenstein, soon to become Liszt's mistress and a fervent worshipper at the shrine of his compositional genius. Within a year she had left her husband and followed Liszt to Weimar, where she spent the next decade as his muse and propagandist. Liszt's dedication to her of his twelve Weimar symphonic poems was no more than her due.

Even while he was still thoroughly occupied as a performer, Liszt had made plans to launch himself as an opera composer. An opera based on Byron's *Corsaire* never got past the planning stage, but the mixed reception of his first *Beethoven Cantata* of 1845, both at its first performance in Bonn and its subsequent repeat in Paris, did not augur well for the future. Nothing daunted, Liszt began to consider another opera, *Sardanapale*, again based on Byron (which came nearer to completion than any other of his projected operas), and continued to jot down ideas in his sketchbooks that were later to form the basis of many of his Weimar orchestral pieces. It would be a mistake to believe that Liszt had gained no orchestral experience in his career up to this time, but with the juvenile opera *Don Sanche* completely forgotten, the *Revolutionary* Symphony simply a bundle of sketches, and the early versions of his piano concerti still in manuscript, Liszt's public profile as a composer was concentrated almost exclusively on solo piano music. Towards the end of 1846 he revealed his frustration to Duke Carl Alexander of Weimar. 'The time has come for me', he declared, 'to break my virtuoso chrysalis and give full flight to my thoughts'.[4]

Liszt's hopes largely centred around *Sardanapale* even as late as 1851, when he eventually abandoned the score after sketching 111 pages of music. An operatic success was the surest way to international acclaim as a composer, and it is still something of a mystery why Liszt should have given up on *Sardanapale* when it was so near to fruition, and when so much of his time was already taken up with opera production in the Weimar theatre. It is possible that Liszt was dissatisfied with even the final version of the *Sardanapale* libretto, which had been the subject of much wrangling with Princess Christina Belgiojoso, who was acting as go-between for an (unidentified) Italian librettist.[5] In addition, Liszt's disenchantment with the quality of the Weimar theatre may have fostered a reluctance to have his own work premièred there. At any rate, after the early 1850s Liszt saw his future mainly as a composer of orchestral music, the Sonata and the *Years of Pilgrimage* having set the seal, as he thought, on his piano works. By 1862, he proudly announced: 'After having, as far as I could, solved the greater part of the *symphonic* problem set me in Germany, I mean now to undertake the *oratorio* problem'.[6] His solution to the troubles of the oratorio was *St Elisabeth*, completed in the same year although planned as far back as 1855, and, finally, *Christus* (1867). The 'symphonic problem' that Liszt also felt confident in having conquered could perhaps be better described as the 'sonata problem' that he addressed pianistically in the Sonata in B minor.

2

Forms and formulae

For Liszt, a large part of the symphonic problem was the future of sonata form after the death of Beethoven. In 1852 he eulogised: 'For us musicians, Beethoven's work is the pillar of cloud and fire which guided the Israelites through the desert – a pillar of cloud to guide us by day, a pillar of fire to guide us by night, *so that we may progress both day and night*'.[1] That same year his pupil Hans von Bülow wrote in the *Neue Zeitschrift für Musik* that the post-Beethoven piano sonata had little to commend it apart from the works of Hummel (the Sonata in F♯ minor), Schumann and Chopin.[2] To be sure, a myriad of sonatas had been published between 1827 and 1852, not least the late sonatas of Schubert and the *Grande sonate* by Alkan, which Liszt would certainly have added to Bülow's roll of honour, but on the whole the form was in decline. The very prestige of Beethoven's reputation had resulted in a plethora of production-line sonatas by younger composers anxious to establish their credentials with an essay in the genre. Schumann summarised the position as it seemed to him in 1839:

We have been long silent respecting achievements in the field of the sonata. Nor have we anything to report today. ... It is remarkable that those who write sonatas are generally unknown men; and it is also strange that the older composers, yet living among us, who grew up in the season of bloom of the sonata, and among whom only Cramer and Moscheles are distinguished, cultivate this form least! It is easy to guess the reason why the former class, generally consisting of young artists, writes them; there exists no better form in which they can introduce themselves and please the higher class of critics, therefore most sonatas of this kind may be regarded as studies in form; they are seldom the result of an irresistible forward impulse.[3]

As a frequent reviewer of new music, Schumann was in a better position than most to witness the nadir of the sonata. In one article he discussed new sonatas by W. Klingenberg, F. A. Lecerf, T. Genischta, W. Taubert and F. Chopin.[4] There are no prizes for guessing which of these was the only one of any interest. In the area of symphonic music a similar situation prevailed, with the honourable exception of Berlioz, and others echoed Schumann's complaint.

'*Forms*', said Liszt, 'were too often changed by quite respectable people into *formulae*'.[5]

A little of the responsibility for this can be placed upon the shoulders of two of Liszt's own teachers: Antonín Reicha and Carl Czerny. Along with Adolf Marx, they were the most influential codifiers of sonata form in the nineteenth century, and it is from their work that we derive the outline of the form now commonly taught in schools and universities. As can be seen from the titles of the treatises – Reicha's *Traité de haute composition musicale* (1826), Marx's *Die Lehre von der musikalischen Komposition* (1845) and Czerny's *School of Practical Composition* (1848) – their aim was to provide a guide for *composers* in the writing of sonata-form movements, rather than musicologists in the analysis of past Classical practice. Their generalisations fit some groups of classical works rather well (Mozart's piano sonatas, for example) and others rather badly (Haydn's symphonies), but they were a powerful influence on the post-Classical generations of composers. This was understandable, for whereas the actual practice of sonata writing in the Classical era was complex and varied, the formulaic scheme as outlined in the treatises was easy and clear cut.

According to Czerny and Reicha, sonata form, defined as the form of the first movement of a sonata or symphony, consisted of three parts: exposition, development and recapitulation. Of these three parts, the exposition was divided from the other two by a double bar, which often included a direction for the whole section to be repeated. The two other sections formed a continuous unit, which was also sometimes, though in the nineteenth century infrequently, repeated. Thus elements of a two-part structure (Reicha's famous *grande coupe binaire*) were superimposed on to the three parts. The exposition presented a 'first-subject' group of melodies in the tonic key joined by a modulating bridge passage to a more lyrical 'second-subject' group in the dominant (or related) key. A closing melody ended the exposition firmly in the new key. The development was tonally unstable, fragmenting and recombining themes already heard before, and led to a recapitulation in which any material initially presented in the dominant key must be repeated in the tonic. This usually required the recomposition of the bridge passage that had originally led to the dominant area, and occasionally the composer took the opportunity to write a second, mini-development section, which, however, went nowhere tonally. Large works followed the recapitulation with a coda, again emphasising the tonic key.

Readers wishing to relate this admittedly simplified plan to actual music should compare it with the opening movement of Mozart's Piano Sonata in

9

A minor, K.310, to which it conforms fairly well, bearing in mind that in minor-key works, the second-subject group was usually in the key of the relative major. Tonally, the essential point to note is that the sonata sets up a polarity between the tonic and dominant key areas in the exposition that is then resolved symmetrically in the recapitulation. In fact, it is quite possible to dispense with the development altogether, creating *slow-movement sonata form*, in which the development is replaced by a few bars of retransition back to the tonic. As the name suggests, this form was rarely found in first movements, and the ingenuity or otherwise of the development section was often dwelled upon by nineteenth-century reviewers of new sonatas. In this context we can understand Liszt's joke that his symphonic poem *Orpheus* was bound to be dismissed with contempt because 'it has no proper *working-out* section!'[6]

It is fairly easy to write composing-by-numbers sonata forms following the Reicha/Czerny scheme – and written they were, in their hundreds. A typical example is the Sonata in C minor, op. 56 (1844), by Liszt's erstwhile rival Sigismond Thalberg, that populariser of the sentimental melody swathed in arpeggios so rightly beloved of café pianists. Thalberg was in reality what Liszt was only caricatured to be: a pianist with considerable talent for arrangement, but with negligible powers of independent invention. In this respect he was the negative of Schumann, who, though a fine composer, had little skill in transcription, as a glance at his Paganini arrangements will confirm. Thalberg's Sonata is by no means the weakest of the Romantic era, but its predictable plan unfolds in relentlessly unvaried four-bar phrases, and gives the undoubtedly correct impression that the piece has been composed out of duty rather than inspiration. Where duty leads enjoyment rarely follows. Thus it is that Thalberg's Sonata op. 56 rests peacefully on library shelves, undisturbed except by writers of books such as this one.

For Liszt, an unthinking and rigid adherence to the sonata-form formula was artistic laziness at its worst, turning music into 'a mere trade'.[7] Again the great example of Beethoven came to his mind. Beethoven's significance lay in his rejection of anything tainted with routine. Liszt saw his output bifurcated into two distinct types:

Were it my place to categorise the different periods of the great master's symphonies and quartets, I should certainly not fix the division into *three styles*, which is now pretty generally adopted ... but, simply recording the questions which have been raised hitherto, I should frankly weigh the *great* question – which is the axis of criticism and of musical aestheticism at the point to which Beethoven has led us – namely, in how far is traditional or recognised form a necessary determinant for the organism of

10

thought? The solution to this question, evolved from the works of Beethoven himself, would lead me to divide his work not into three styles or periods … but quite logically into two categories: the first, that in which traditional and recognised form contains and governs the thought of the master, and the second, that in which the thought stretches, breaks, re-creates and fashions the form and style according to its needs and inspirations … in the domain of the Beautiful, Genius alone is the authority.[8]

Most of Liszt's creative efforts in Weimar were concentrated on following Beethoven's lead – particularly in the rejuvenation of sonata form. Although he did not specify in the letter quoted above which works of Beethoven fell into the second, novel, category, indubitably one of the most influential on his general approach to sonata form was the finale of the Ninth Symphony. In this variation movement we find the germ of so many Lisztian traits. The variations are organised as a large-scale sonata structure in D major, with the 'second subject' a transformation of the main theme into a Turkish march in B♭ (the flattened submediant); then comes a fugal development followed by a recapitulation. The recapitulation is interrupted by a slow section, based on a new theme, initially in the subdominant. In fact, this slow section is analogous to the secondary development section sometimes found in recapitulations. Its theme is immediately taken up again, in the tonic, as a glorious counterpoint to the principal *Ode to Joy* melody for the second, and by far the larger, section of the recapitulation. If we consider the march as a scherzo-substitute, we have all the ingredients of a four-movement work bound up in one, and underpinned by the use of thematic transformation. This in essence is what is often given as a description of the Liszt Sonata, although there are important differences in detail.

The idea of encapsulating elements of several movements in one might be considered fundamentally Beethovenian, but already by 1822 Schubert in his *Wanderer* Fantasy had successfully achieved the same feat. The *Wanderer* Fantasy was one of Liszt's favourite concert-pieces, which he arranged for piano and orchestra in 1851. Many fantasies, for example those of Beethoven and Hummel, or even Kalkbrenner's dilapidated *Effusio musica*, are composed of short, contrasting sections in a variety of keys and tempi. Schubert, however, follows a more complex plan, using thematic transformation to link sections together in a scheme of first section (C major), slow section (C♯ minor–E major), scherzo (A♭ major) and finale (C major, beginning with a fugal exposition). We can see, incidentally, from this description how mistaken are those commentators who attribute the 'invention' of thematic transformation – which is, anyway, only a type of variation of ancient pedigree – to Liszt.

By the age of thirteen Liszt had learned that it was possible to accommodate sections of varied characters within a basic sonata structure. His *Impromptu on themes of Rossini and Spontini* of 1824 is organised in this way, with the Rossini themes appearing as a sonata exposition and recapitulation, while the Spontini themes form an interlude in the centre of the piece. Of course, to compare the *Impromptu* with Schubert's *Wanderer* Fantasy or Beethoven's Ninth Symphony is like comparing a whelk to a whale, but it does show that even in this youthful work Liszt was experimenting with sonata variants in one movement. The idea that an important piece could consist of one movement alone, and not three or four, seemed to have particular appeal to him. In a review written in 1837 of some of Schumann's piano music, and discussing in particular the sonata Schumann had entitled *Concerto without Orchestra*, Liszt mused over the history of concerto form.[9] Previously a concerto had to have three movements, he opined. John Field, however, in his Concerto No. 7, had replaced the second solo section of the first movement with an Adagio, Moscheles in his *Concert fantastique*, op. 90, had united the three movements into one, and Weber, Mendelssohn and Herz had also proceeded along this path. The future lay in free treatment of traditional form, a future that his own music was to embrace enthusiastically.

Schumann, for his part, had also been stimulated into some musical clairvoyance by Moscheles' *Concert fantastique*. In a discussion of Moscheles' work he seems to be acting as a reluctant prophet for the Liszt Sonata, although his description of a one-movement piece could apply equally well to the already written *Wanderer* Fantasy, or to the first movement of his own Piano Concerto in A minor, originally intended as an independent piece.

The *Concert fantastique* consists of four movements, continued without pause, but in different degrees of time. We have already declared ourselves opposed to this form. Though it does not seem impossible to construct an agreeable whole in it, yet the aesthetic dangers appear too great in comparison with this possibility. Still, there is a lack of smaller concert pieces, in which the virtuoso can give us, at the same time, his performance of an allegro, adagio and rondo. It would be well to invent a new one, to consist of one great movement in moderate tempo, within which form the preparatory passage might take the place of a first allegro, the cantabile that of an adagio, and a brilliant close might replace a rondo. Perhaps this idea may suggest something which we would gladly see embodied in a peculiar original composition. The movement might well be written for pianoforte alone.[10]

Although there were precedents for concerti and fantasies in one continuous movement, there was none for the piano sonata. Liszt's approach in the B minor Sonata could be broadly described as a marriage of the fantasy, which

12

was normally in one movement, with the traditional sonata. Beethoven, of course, had again shown the way with his two sonatas 'quasi una fantasia', op. 27. These sonatas are directed to be played without a break between movements. Op. 27 no. 1 is especially notable in this regard in that the movements themselves are not independent, unlike op. 27 no. 2, from which the first movement is so often excerpted that many think it alone constitutes the famous *Moonlight* Sonata. Individual movements in op. 27 no. 1 are further linked by thematic connections (most obviously that of the initial falling third) and by the recall of the Adagio movement just before the close of the piece. This cyclical recall was to become a favourite device of many Romantic composers, and is also a feature of Beethoven's later sonata op. 101. Liszt performed both op. 27 sonatas frequently, the latter perhaps too frequently, and neatly inverted their title for the final version of *Après une lecture du Dante*, which he described as a *Fantasia quasi sonata*. This work will be discussed in more detail later, but here it will be enough to note that despite the title, the *Dante* Sonata is in a fairly strict sonata form, and is actually less like a fantasy than Beethoven's op. 27 no. 1.

Of course the term 'fantasy' itself need imply no particular form at all, and when used in connection with *Après une lecture du Dante* is perhaps as much a reflection of the febrile content than anything else. Schumann vacillated for some time over the title of his own *Fantasy* op. 17, dedicated to Liszt. An earlier version of the piece was to be called *Sonata for Beethoven*. Unusually for a fantasy, the work is in three distinct movements, with the ghost of Beethoven's sonata op. 101 hovering over certain elements, such as the dominant pedal opening of the first movement (with a subsequent half-cadence on the submediant minor) and the stern dotted-rhythms of the sequences in the march, decorated with forceful right-hand trills. Of the influence of Beethoven's own free and wild *Fantasy*, op. 77, there is not a trace. Beethoven's op. 101 seems to have held a special place in the affections of both Schumann and Mendelssohn; Mendelssohn's Sonata in E starts with a crib from it, and its influence on the Schumann *Fantasy* would tell us that at one time Schumann considered the work in relation to a sonata archetype, even if we did not know of the original title.

Liszt was a fervent admirer of the Schumann *Fantasy*, which he considered a work of the highest quality; he was openly proud to be the dedicatee. Though the first movement of the *Fantasy* has some resemblance to sonata form, the key relationships are highly unusual: a second group in F major (the subdominant) recapitulated in E♭ (the flat mediant). In other words, contrary to the Classical principles of moving from the tonic key to a key of greater tension (the dominant), Schumann moves to a key of lesser tension for the second group, which is then recapitulated in a non-tonic key. The tonal functions of exposition and recapitulation seem all awry here, at least by Classical standards.[11] The position of the central *Im Legendenton* section of the *Fantasy's* first movement has also been the cause of much scholarly anxiety – is it an interlude within the development or within the recapitulation? In fact, so much of the form of Schumann's *Fantasy* is deliberately ambiguous that there is no concrete answer one way or the other. That the question has been raised at all at least shows that the *Fantasy* does not fall into the dreary catalogue of formulaic music that Liszt railed against. Indeed, the formal subtlety of the work was an inspiration to Liszt in designing the Mephistophelean ambiguities of his own Sonata (does its fugue form part of the development or the recapitulation?).

It is not surprising that the tonal layout of the Schumann *Fantasy* has so little resemblance to traditional sonata form, for this aspect of the sonata – which some might argue was the most important – posed particular difficulties for the Romantics. A sonata sets up a tonal polarity, or tension, in the exposition, between the tonic and dominant, which is then resolved symmetrically in the recapitulation by the presentation *in the tonic* of any material originally introduced in the dominant key. Indeed, the tonic recapitulation of non-tonic material is one of the few defining features of sonata form in general. Romantic composers, whose musical material was gradually becoming more chromatic and less firmly grounded in one key, often found the long tonic anchor required in the recapitulation inimical to their musical style. The exposition presented similar problems.

In music which normally utilised wide-ranging chromaticism, an exposition modulation to the dominant or relative major seemed as tame to the 1840s as the shocks of a 1950s Hammer Horror film to the 1990s. A mediant modulation was much more congenial and effective to Romantic composers than the simple dominant, and indeed Beethoven had used the mediant key for the second group frequently, from the *Waldstein* Sonata onwards. Liszt followed the tonal plan of the *Waldstein* in the symphonic poem *Les préludes*. Beethoven, however, retained the relative major as the usual key for the second group for works in the minor, an approach which the next generation largely followed. Unfortunately for a composer like Chopin this could be a sticking point. Chopin's music often fluctuates naturally between a minor key and its relative major. Several passages of the Ballade in A♭, for example, occupy ambiguous ground between A♭ major and F minor, the same is true for the B♭ minor/D♭ major of the second scherzo. In the Sonata, op. 35, the move from B♭ minor to the second group in D♭ major hardly seems like a modulation at all. Chopin attempts to dramatise the transition by a sudden halt and abrupt change of movement, but only succeeds in making life more difficult for the interpreter, who has to decide how to make the whole piece sound convincing.

For his third Sonata, op. 58, Chopin adopted a scheme used by Hummel in his Sonata in F♯ minor, op. 81, namely a highly chromatic transition hinting at various distant keys (in this case B♭ major and E♭) before a long period on the dominant of the relative major establishes it as the true second key. By this means any memory of the tonic key is effaced, and the relative major appears satisfyingly exotic. (The procedure is identical to an unscrupulous taxi-driver taking tourists for a five-mile saunter around town to a destination that is in reality only two hundred yards away.) Liszt, who admired and performed both Chopin's and Hummel's sonatas, uses a similar procedure in the Sonata in B minor. This is unusual in his work of the 1850s. In the symphonies and symphonic poems that are minor-key sonata forms he normally modulates to the key a major third above the tonic for the second group, as if the tonic itself were major – the first movement of the *Faust* Symphony is a case in point (C minor/E major).

That we can write at all about Liszt's normal sonata procedure may be a surprise to some, who consider that most of his music unfolds in some amorphous Romantic manner with scarcely any relation to traditional formal types. For this misunderstanding Liszt himself is partly to blame. He talked so volubly about freeing music from the shackles of conventional form, about moulding form anew for each piece depending on the content, and about programmatic inspiration, that we might be forgiven for dismissing sonata form as largely irrelevant to his music. In fact there are many Liszt 'sonatas' both for piano and for orchestra.

Liszt had already written three solo piano sonatas in 1825 at the age of fourteen, and one was composed soon after for piano duet.[12] These were unpublished and are now lost. In later life Liszt was asked about them by his biographer Lina Ramann, and in a fit of nostalgia copied from memory the opening page of one, in F minor. This begins with the same harmonic progression as Beethoven's *Moonlight* Sonata, but beyond that shows no more sign of profundity than the prolix *Rondo* and *Allegro di bravura*, published around the same time. Liszt made a note of the first three bars of another of the sonatas, in C minor, in a letter to his mother of 1836, in which he asked her to send him all his juvenile pieces.[13] These three bars tell us nothing about the work, except that it was no tragic loss to posterity. Themes from Liszt's juvenilia occasionally turn up in his later music. The introduction to the

15

Impromptu on themes of Rossini and Spontini, mentioned earlier as being in a loose sonata form, reappears in maturer guise as the opening flourish of the transcendental study *Eroica,* and the recently published 'Concerto No. 3' is a patchwork of such self-borrowing. Who can tell if anything survives in this way from the three sonatas? In any event, Liszt was not as precocious as Mozart or Mendelssohn in his compositional development. Fluent though his youthful music might be, it always prompts the qualification 'for someone of that age'.

Liszt himself was under no illusions about the quality of his early compositional efforts. In old age he remarked that his infant composing and improvising was hampered by the small stretch of his hands, but any notes he couldn't reach he often managed to strike with his nose – an uncanny premonition of some of the more avant-garde twentieth-century performance styles. The fact that his sonatas remained unpublished while sets of meretricious variations were offered to the public shows that the main purpose of his juvenile music was to display an already brilliant keyboard technique. The only record we have of a performance of one of the sonatas is a concert in Bordeaux in 1826. With hardened cynicism, Liszt told the audience that the piece was by Beethoven, and laughed inwardly as his listeners fell into raptures over its sublime merits. A few years later in Paris he pulled a similar trick, swapping trios by Beethoven and Pixis. Pixis himself could not suppress a smile when he saw his own fairly pedestrian music mistaken for that of Beethoven and eulogised accordingly. Needless to say, the real Beethoven piece, labouring under its false identity, was found to be dull and vapid. Of all Liszt's early keyboard music the Scherzo in G minor of 1827 is perhaps the most prophetic of future greatness, partly because its acerbic humour seems to spring from the same sardonic attitude as the concert: counterfeiting.

The next decade saw the burgeoning of Liszt's creative genius. Sometime in the first half of the 1830s he composed the so-called *Duo (Sonata)* for violin and piano in four movements and based on Chopin's Mazurka in C♯ minor, op. 6 no. 2. He wisely did not choose to publish this bizarre and rambling work, which remained in manuscript until 1964, but his interest in sonata form reawakened for several of the *Douze grandes études* of 1837 and for the first version of *Vallée d'Obermann,* in *Album d'un Voyageur.* The original *Vallée* is a monothematic sonata movement in E minor with a rhapsodic introduction based on three descending notes, G–F♯–E. The entire piece is developed from this figure, which is expanded to create a first-subject theme reminiscent of that of the first movement of Weber's Sonata in E minor. A second group in the relative major consists of a *dolcissimo con amore* transformation of the theme again similar to the Weber, which obviously constituted a potent background model. The fiery development initially elaborates music from the introduction, eventually leading into a long recapitulation in E minor/ major. In all, the last eight pages of an eighteen-page piece are in E, and by the time we reach the end we might feel we've had enough tonic stability to last some time.

Liszt recast this work radically in the 1850s, turning it into one of his most sublime achievements. Many of the problems with the earlier version can be traced to its almost pedantic sonata structure. The close similarity of the exposition and recapitulation fatally weakens the effect of the latter, while the long anchor on the tonic key engenders a feeling of tedium rather than resolution. In the later version resemblances to a sonata layout are far more distant. Among other changes, there is no recapitulation of the main theme in the minor; instead the major mode appears immediately after the central development, to incomparably greater effect. The exposition too is recomposed. Liszt replaces the relative major with the submediant major (C), juxtaposing it starkly with the initial E minor. Again the result is deeply moving in a way that eluded the early version. The new *Vallée d'Obermann* is no longer so obviously a sonata, but, rather more importantly, it has become a great piece of music.

As mentioned before, the 1837 *Douze grandes études* have their final version in the Transcendental Studies of 1851. In both collections the C minor, F minor and D♭ major studies are sonata designs. The 1837 C minor study is monothematic – all second-subject material is developed from the first subject. Liszt creates a second group of dual character, one section based on the jagged chordal figure of bars 2–3, the other a lyrical theme spun out from the descending scale of bar 1. Again the second tonality is the relative major, recapitulated in the tonic major. It was this long recapitulation that was drastically pruned in the 1851 version; the return of the first group in the minor was eliminated altogether, and the recapitulation now started with the second group in the tonic major. The parallels with *Vallée d'Obermann* are compelling, not just in monothematicism and tonality, but also in Liszt's revision procedures as they affect the recapitulation. The dual nature of the second group in the C minor study is, moreover, a significant novelty in Liszt's output up to that time. We shall find a similar approach in the B minor Sonata.

The chief interest of the F minor study – apart from the obvious fact that it contains some of the best music in the set - is that here Liszt breaks away from a reliance on the relative major as contrasting key. Now we have the distinctly iconoclastic key of the flattened leading-note minor (E♭ minor). This

17

is no mere academic point. E♭ minor is a key of lesser tension relative to F minor, and placing the second group in this tonality noticeably increases the depressive mood of the music. Liszt obviously took this exact key scheme from the first movement of his beloved *Moonlight* Sonata, but the *Appassionata* Sonata too was a potent model. The link with the *Appassionata* is most evident in the 1837 version, in which we find a *Presto feroce* coda modelled on that of Beethoven's Sonata. Liszt largely excised this in 1851, leaving only the similarity between the main theme of the study and that of Chopin's op.10 no. 9 as a tribute to external influence. The use of a second group entirely in the minor is, of course, highly unusual in terms of Classical practice, but frequent later on in Brahms's output.

The D♭ major study is scarcely less original in its tonal construction. Here the second key is E major (flattened mediant), but the surprise lies in the polytonal overlay of the first group. Consistent polytonality in a first group is impossible in conventional sonata form, for there would be no way of establishing a tonic key. Liszt's first group here is firmly rooted in D♭ major by the bass (which merely swings between the tonic and dominant notes), but the right hand strews chords hinting at E major over this solid foundation, anticipating the eventual arrival of the second group. The impressionistic effect created is a stroke of genius decades ahead of its time. Needless to say, all this requires an unusually massive confirmation of D♭ in the recapitulation, which we duly get, heralded in the 1837 version by a gargantuan dominant pedal (Allegro vivace).

The sonata form of these three *Grandes études* was a new feature of their 1837 rewriting. The very first version, the *Etudes en douze exercices* of 1826, is entirely devoid of sonata form, save perhaps in the central modulation to E major of the C minor study, which is prophetic of Liszt's later favourite second-group key area. Of course, when Liszt turned this into a fully fledged sonata movement in 1837 he forsook E major as a second key for the more conservative relative major. It is important to note that none of the revisions made in 1837 had anything to do with programmaticism. The familiar titles, *Wilde Jagd* (Wild Hunt) for the C minor study and *Harmonies du soir* for the D♭, only appeared in the Weimar final version. Even in this version the F minor study remained devoid of title, as did the A minor, which some have suggested calling 'Paganini' because of its violinistic leaps. Only the D minor study *Mazeppa* was published under that name before 1851, in a separate edition with a dedication to Victor Hugo and a new ending. This ending is indeed programmatic, representing Mazeppa's final triumph after his nightmarish ride across the steppes, but it is the only example of material

18

added to the studies for programmatic reasons. However apt the titles may appear, they were in most cases devised nearly twenty-five years after the initial conception of the music. Paradoxically, discussion of the studies, taking its cue from the titles, has often concentrated on supposedly descriptive elements in the music, at the expense of its formal ingenuity. The sheer keyboard imagination they display has always been recognised, and was acknowledged even by the contemporary critic Fétis, a one-time partisan of Liszt's rival Thalberg. Fétis could hardly have failed to applaud the G major study (*Vision* in 1851), a tribute to (or parody of) Thalberg's famous arpeggio writing in his ubiquitous *Moses* Fantasy.

We can see from the foregoing that, in his earlier music, Liszt found sonata form most congenial when he allowed himself some liberty with the usual tonal and harmonic procedures. Both the *Vallée d'Obermann* and the C minor study seem less successful in their first versions, partly because of a rather tame tonal layout and a too literal recapitulation. The revisions take a leaf out of Chopin's sonatas and omit the first-group recapitulation, with great advantage to the music's sustained interest.

The first version of the *Dante* Sonata was written, too, in the late 1830s, entitled *Fragment nach Dante*, but the piece now played is chiefly the result of a revision in 1849, and of further changes made before its eventual publication in 1858 in the Italian volume of *Years of Pilgrimage*, there called *Après une lecture du Dante*, from the eponymous poem by Victor Hugo. *Fragment nach Dante* was in two thematically related parts. The 1849 revision conflates these parts into a single-movement sonata form. The *Dante* Sonata evinces the tonal layout common to many of the symphonic poem sonata forms of Liszt's Weimar years: a minor key first group followed by a second group in the raised mediant major (D minor/F♯ major). A striking feature of the work is the use of a tonally dislocating tritone figure (first heard opening the piece) as part of the main thematic material. This tritone figure recurs at major structural points, and thus functions in a similar way to the opening descending-scale theme of the Sonata in B minor. There is, too, a second group derived from first-subject material, that itself was initially adumbrated in the slow introduction. As in the D♭ major study, the restless chromaticism of the first subject (Presto agitato assai) only affects the upper voices – the bass closely hugs the tonic key of D minor. It should be emphasised that there is nothing particularly programmatic about the *structure* of the *Dante* Sonata (as opposed to the character of the themes) apart from the general outline. The struggle–triumph trajectory that Liszt follows here is common to a great number of his works. Indeed he deliberately chose 'subjects' that could be interpreted in this manner – Prometheus, Obermann, Faust, Tasso and other suffering, yet ultimately victorious characters. Such an emotional course is easily fitted to a minor-key sonata form with a recapitulation in the tonic major, although obviously other forms are possible like *Mazeppa*, which follows the tonic minor–major plan with few sonata tendencies.

The first step towards an expanded sonata form was the rather unimaginatively named *Grand Concert-solo* in E minor of 1849. This must be the only large-scale work of Liszt for which no one has suggested a hitherto unimagined 'programme', perhaps because it has never been well enough known to attract the fabulist's attention. A distant model was Chopin's *Fantasy* in F minor, a loose sonata form with a slow section interpolated between development and recapitulation. Liszt's *Concert-solo* follows a similar plan, with a firmer sonata outline. The work has often been considered a preliminary sketch for the Sonata in B minor, partly because of its structure and partly because a member of the first group of themes bears a strong resemblance to a theme in the Sonata (Sonata theme 2, see page 35). This is one of Liszt's favourite melodic tags, which also makes an appearance in the *Faust* Symphony, among other works. The transformation of another first-group theme into a Grandioso second subject (in the relative major) also recalls the Sonata, although in the latter the Grandioso melody is new. A central slow section (Andante sostenuto) consists of three varied statements of a sentimental Db major/F minor theme. (Unfortunately the evident kinship between this and the slow theme of Chopin's *Fantasy* painfully points up the inferiority of the former.) The recapitulation includes a funeral-march transformation of the Grandioso theme, and a return of the Andante Sostenuto in the tonic major before a closing peroration based on the Grandioso. The parallels between the original coda of the B minor Sonata and the end of the *Concert-solo* are significant, as is the identity of the tempo designations: Allegro energico – Grandioso – Andante sostenuto – Allegro energico. Yet again, the necessity of a long area of tonic stability in the recapitulation causes problems for Liszt, who appears momentarily unable to think of a way of retaining interest along with E major. In his reworking of the piece for two pianos as *Concerto pathétique* (1856), he cut the Gordian knot by simply transposing a large chunk of the recapitulation down a semitone into Eb major. This certainly makes for more variety, and should be considered by performers of the solo version.

Commissioned by the Paris Conservatoire as a test piece for a piano competition, the *Concert-solo* was originally written without the slow section. In its original conception, the work was in a relatively conventional sonata form. Liszt sketched out an arrangement for piano and orchestra of this version before deciding to make major additions to the piece. By the time he came to write the Sonata in B minor, the experience of composing the *Concert-solo* and related works helped him to conceive of a slow section as part of the original inspiration. The *Concert-solo* has always languished in the shadow of the Sonata, and has received far fewer performances than its quality deserves, despite being championed by Liszt's pupils Tausig and von Bülow. Von Bülow even published his own edition of the two-piano version, adding a long cadenza before the coda. Liszt admired Bülow's reworking, and also took a close interest in the new arrangement of the *Concert-solo* for piano and orchestra by Edward Reuss, eventually published long after Liszt's death in 1896. Liszt devoted a large amount of time to revising Reuss's arrangement, which had been sent to him during his last stay in Rome. Part of the manuscript of his alterations to Reuss's work is at present lost, but so many of Liszt's 'lost' manuscripts have recently turned up that we might harbour some hope for the eventual recovery of the rest, after which it will no doubt be sold to an anonymous buyer for a vast sum of money and disappear again.

Soon after finishing the *Concert-solo* Liszt composed the magnificent *Fantasy and Fugue on 'Ad nos, ad salutarem undam'* for organ, a monothematic sonata analogue in which the fugue begins the recapitulation and a slow section again fulfils some of the functions of a development.[14] Unlike the Sonata in B minor, the slow section is tonally remote from the outer parts of the work, its F♯ major in a tritone relationship to the basic tonic of C minor. The sense of distance is emphasised by the slow section beginning with the only complete, unadorned statement in the whole piece of Meyerbeer's chorale theme. (For some unaccountable reason, Busoni omits this passage from his otherwise splendid solo piano arrangement.) Few pieces give a better idea of Liszt's advanced chromatic language than the *Fantasy and Fugue*. In the opening pages the theme is presented in a variety of complex harmonisations over a tonic pedal. As each phrase ends inconclusively on a dissonant chord the music is propelled forward, seeking a harmonic resolution it never attains, in increasingly baffled frustration. This deliberate avoidance of tonal closure is far from the normal exposition procedures of sonata form, but we find similar harmonic evasions in the opening two pages of the B minor Sonata, before the first full confirmation of the tonic key. It is easy to see from this music why Wagner found Liszt's harmonic style so important for the development of his yearning *Tristan* chromaticism.

The *Scherzo and March* (1851), published just after the Sonata, makes use of elements of sonata form in a creative and novel manner. The first Scherzo section is a sonata form with a second group in the dominant minor (D minor

– A minor), the prevalence of the minor mode contributing to the bleak and demonic atmosphere. The main theme of the second group again recalls theme 2 of the Sonata in B minor. The development treats this theme fugally (like the Sonata) before it is eventually recapitulated in the tonic minor. The March (in B♭ major) takes the place of the trio of the Scherzo, which is then repeated in varied form only up to the middle of the exposition (where the music originally began its move to A minor). A starkly powerful coda brings back the March theme and the Scherzo octave theme as a virtuoso whirlwind in D. It is surprising that this superb and rewarding work has been so neglected by pianists, and often dismissed by writers. The *Scherzo and March* was Liszt's final pianistic preparation for the Sonata in B minor, and his last backward glance at the *Moonlight* Sonata, in the third movement of which we find the same tonic–dominant minor-key scheme. His claim that Beethoven was 'the pillar of cloud and fire' guiding him through the musical desert was thus no empty boast.

Orchestral sonata forms

Beethoven was a similarly powerful influence on Liszt's Weimar orchestral music, most of which shows him again bringing his fertile musical intellect to bear on the 'sonata problem'. As is so often the case with Liszt, the chronology of the symphonic poems is very difficult to disentangle. Though all published after the Sonata, many were composed long before it, at least in their early versions. *Héroïde funèbre* was conceived as far back as 1830 as a movement for a *Revolutionary* Symphony, but was revised towards the beginning of Liszt's Weimar period to become the magnificent elegy published a few years later. *Héroïde Funèbre* is a funeral march in sonata form, with an exposition key scheme of F minor – D♭ major, the second group (the 'trio' of the march) recapitulated in the tonic major. Like the Sonata in B minor, the first theme makes use of the Hungarian gypsy scale, in this case probably a reference to the bloody events of the recent Hungarian Revolution (1848). A reference to the 'Marseillaise' has its origin in the first sketches of the work written during the Paris July Revolution of 1830. Towards the end of the piece a long build up of diminished-seventh chords over a pedal bass, in the midst of which are strewn fragments of the first-subject theme, is an evident allusion to the hushed expectancy of 'über Sternen muss er wohnen' in the *Ode to Joy* of Beethoven's Ninth Symphony. To a listener who knows the extent of the slaughter in the Hungarian Revolution, the allusion to the Beethoven, with its confidence in a heavenly Father dwelling above the stars, might seem deliberately ironic. The sincerity of Liszt's religious faith can, however, never be in doubt. If a specific reference was intended here, it was surely only musical.

Of the other orchestral works written before the Sonata, *Les préludes* and *Prometheus* are unproblematic sonata forms. As mentioned before, *Les préludes* follows the key scheme of Beethoven's *Waldstein* Sonata. *Prometheus* is more typically Lisztian, with a minor-key first group (A minor) followed by a lyrical second group in the raised mediant major (D♭ major). The introduction is in effect a thematic catalogue, and the tonic key is not properly defined until the entry of the *allegro* first-subject group (as in the Sonata in B minor). A fugue forms most of the development, while the recapitulation is prefaced by a varied reprise of the introduction. The use of the introduction as a repository of embryonic themes, later to be developed in fuller form, and a reappearance to articulate the main division of the work became increasingly congenial to Liszt. As his sonata forms expanded, taking in elements of slow and scherzo movements, he became more concerned with their structural clarity. In the B minor Sonata, theme 1 performs a similar function to the introduction reprise in other works: indicating important sectional divisions. The approach in the Sonata is, however, more subtle than in *Prometheus*, thrilling though that work that is.

Liszt probably first got the idea of repeating part of the introduction later in the work from Beethoven's *Pathétique* Sonata, but it is certainly a common feature of his operatic fantasies, where introductions are often treated as ritornellos, reappearing later to divide one opera theme from another. A fantasy such as that on Donizetti's *Lucrezia Borgia* (second part) not only uses an introduction, but one formed out of fragments of the main melodies – the thematic catalogue approach so common in Liszt's 'original' music. Liszt was evidently using these virtuoso works as compositional testing-grounds for his later music, a fact that would be more frequently recognised if a stirring piece like the *Lucrezia Borgia* Fantasy were more often played (or rather was ever played). The kinship between Liszt's opera fantasies and his sonata-form music can be further illustrated by his later fantasies on Wagner's *Rienzi* and Gounod's *Faust Waltz*, which are, in effect, sonatas in tonal construction.

The first sketches for *Ce qu'on entend sur la montagne* were made in 1848, but Liszt had such problems with the piece that publication was delayed for nearly a decade. As a result it is best considered along with *Die Ideale* as an example of the expanded sonata form Liszt originally perfected in the Sonata in B minor. *Tasso, Lamento e trionfo*, too, did not reach its final form until after the composition of the Sonata, although Liszt had composed at least two versions (not counting the piano piece from the first *Venezia e Napoli* in which he set the main theme) before 1852.

Tasso follows a similar tonal scheme to the '*ad nos*': two outer sections in C, with a central episode – in this case a minuet – in F♯ major. Like the *Fantasy and Fugue* it is monothematic, all the musical material being derived from the Venetian gondolier's song heard as the first subject in C minor. A second group in E major proves simply to be a transformation of the first subject, which is also presented in varied form for the recapitulation in C major (the *Trionfo*). Where we might expect a development section we find the minuet, again based on the gondolier's song, and the whole piece is articulated by two reprises of the introduction. This introduction is itself in ABA' form, the B episode in a faster Allegro energico tempo, contrasting with the Lento of the two A episodes. The A part of the introduction returns, varied, before the minuet, and the rest makes its appearance before the *Trionfo* recapitulation. Paradoxically, this chain of introduction repeats that Liszt thought helped to render the form of *Tasso* comprehensible has been responsible for a large measure of confusion among analysts. Many interpret the Allegro energico of the introduction as some sort of inept first subject and then proceed to be puzzled by the rest of the music, falling back on the old complaint about Liszt's 'loose' episodic structures. The reason why the introduction – including the Allegro energico – cannot be anything but introductory is that tonally it functions as a large-scale dominant preparation for the C minor first subject. Liszt's stroke of genius is to have a slow minor-key exposition subject (the *Lamento*) recapitulated in a fast major-key variation (the *Trionfo*). To fully understand the organisation of a work like *Tasso*, we always have to keep the idea of sonata form in mind, as Liszt's innovations derive from a basic sonata blueprint. This might have been easier for audiences at performances of early versions of the piece. *Tasso*, and some other of the symphonic poems, were originally performed as concert overtures, a title that usually gave rise to the expectation of a piece in sonata form.

From *Tasso* and *Prometheus* we can try to build up a picture of basic elements of a Liszt Weimar sonata form: an introduction in varied tempi containing fragments of some of the main themes, or, in the case of a monothematic work, a selection of motifs from the central theme; further repeats of part of this introduction at important formal divisions of the work; a second group in the (raised) mediant major; pervasive thematic transformation throughout the work; and an emotional path from anguished despair to exalted triumph. Of course, as Liszt was anxious never to fall into any compositional routine an attempt to strictly define his compositional approach is doomed to failure.

Héroïde funèbre, for example, displays none of the features listed above, while *Les préludes* could truly be said to have only two (a second group in the mediant major and pervasive thematic transformation). Particularly relevant to the Sonata in B minor, however, is the replacing of a central development in *Tasso* with a minuet, analogous to the placing of a slow section within its development.

The structure of *Ce qu'on entend sur la montagne* is even larger than the Sonata, exhibiting a massive three-key exposition going from E♭ major to the lowered mediant F♯ and finally landing on the conventional dominant of B♭. This is a huge expansion of a tonal scheme found in the first movement of Beethoven's *Emperor* Concerto, and further elaborated in Schubert's last piano sonata. The sheer length of the development requires that it be clearly divided off – two repeated episodes stand like pillars at its beginning and end – and the whole work plays in one continuous movement for around thirty minutes, similar to the timing of the Sonata. *Ce qu'on entend* represents Liszt's most ambitious inflation of the single-movement sonata structure, though the 'scherzo' element that we find in the Sonata in B minor is less obvious as a discrete section.

Die Ideale, however, does display a 'slow section' – 'scherzo' sequence at the heart of what is again a modified sonata form, both sections interlinked by thematic transformation. Beethoven's *Coriolan* Overture was a powerful influence on the treatment of the second group in the exposition of this symphonic poem. Liszt fervently admired the overture as one of Beethoven's most daring works, and it certainly contains many fascinating features, including a subdominant recapitulation, and a restless second group that never quite settles in any one key, its theme extended in a modulatory sequence. *Die Ideale* adopts the latter feature on a larger scale, the second group moving languidly in separate blocks through the keys of D, B and E, like panels on a triptych. Thematically, the second group is closely related to the first, and indeed the melodic kernel of the entire piece can be found in the introduction. As we might expect, this introduction is partially repeated before the slow section, which is positioned as part of a long development. The placing of the slow and scherzo episodes in C♯ minor, sounding a major third below the tonic of F, is only one of the many third relationships that pervade this work, both tonally and melodically.

Tonal structure based on thirds is a staple of Romantic music, and rarely more frequently encountered than in Liszt's Weimar compositions. The second group of the graceful *Orpheus* (1853–4) is in the expected major-third relation (C major – E major) as is that of the first movement of the 1854 *Faust*

Symphony (C minor – E major). (The first movement of the *Faust* Symphony, like *Tasso*, also features a tripartite introduction, reprised later at the centre of the development.) The B minor Sonata, then, and its predecessor the *Concert-solo*, are unusual in retaining the conventional key of the relative major for the second group instead of Liszt's favourite raised mediant. The only other sonata form of this period that is equally conventional is the symphonic poem *Festklänge* (*Festival Sounds*), written, significantly, just after the Sonata in 1853.

Festklänge begins with a dual-tempo introduction presenting important motifs in various 'wrong' keys. The *allegro* first-subject group is in C major, continuing on its boisterous path to reach the chord of B major, seemingly as dominant preparation for a second group in E. Liszt, however, springs a surprise by treating B, not as a dominant of E, but as the bass of an augmented-sixth chord that soon lands us in G minor/major, in which key the second group unfolds. A second group in the dominant appears positively archaic, but Liszt's preparation for it has played subtly on the expectation of a more distant tonal ramble. As if to underline the joke, the climax of the second group glances at E major, only to be hijacked by another augmented-sixth chord and plumped firmly back into G, like an errant child (bars 193–200). The skill with which Liszt carries off this witty tonal sleight of hand is surely owing, in part, to his experience with a similar approach in the Sonata in B minor a few months earlier.

Liszt's other Weimar orchestral pieces have a more distant relation to the sonata archetype. The beautiful *Gretchen* movement from the *Faust* Symphony eschews tonal contrast almost entirely for its opening section, presenting two main subjects in the same key (A♭ major). This serves to emphasise the reappearance of Faust's themes in the middle section of the movement, when the tonality is suddenly wrenched into C minor. Although a tonic recapitulation closes the movement, tonal polarity is so essential in the exposition of a sonata that we can hardly describe *Gretchen* as being in that form. (The adolescent Chopin, however, was of a different opinion. The opening exposition of his first Sonata does not modulate either, to rather unhappy effect.) The symphonic poem *Mazeppa* is a conflation of two earlier pieces – the eponymous Transcendental Study and the *Arbeiterchor* – with no connection with sonata form. *Hungaria* and *Hamlet* are both novel structures, the latter an ingenious and tautly written arch-form; the former showing only tenuous connections with sonata practice. Also distantly related is the first movement of the *Dante* Symphony. Like *Gretchen*, this movement is in an ABA form, with both outer sections based in one key, in this case D. Contrast is nevertheless achieved in the 'A' section analogous to that of a sonata exposition by the inspired transformation of restlessly chromatic thematic material (a 'first group') into more diatonic versions (a 'second group'), the whole always centred around D. This procedure had an important influence on several twentieth-century composers, such as Skryabin and Bartók.

From this overview, we can see that Liszt's Sonata in B minor, far from being an isolated example of sonata form in an oeuvre otherwise teeming with programmatic 'free' forms, is in fact one of a vast family of Lisztian sonatas. Liszt's preoccupation with the example of Beethoven could hardly have had any other result, for his claim to be following Beethoven's lead was not empty propaganda, and necessarily drew him towards the formal type most characteristic of the great master. One of the ironies of Romantic music in Germany is that both major factions – the 'Music of the Future' grouping of Liszt and Wagner, and the traditionalist composers centring later around Brahms – saw themselves as spiritual children of Beethoven. If for a long time this obscured the more progressive elements in Brahms, it similarly obscured Liszt's respect for musical tradition, caricaturing him as a crude iconoclast. In Liszt's case the myth has survived longer. Only when we realise how much the Music of the Future stood on the shoulders of the past can we comprehend Liszt's true innovative genius.

3

Understanding the Sonata in B minor

As a musician anxious to avoid formulaic composition, Liszt surely would have been delighted at the amount of scholarly bickering engendered by the Sonata in B minor. Such dissension is usually caused by the tendency of analysts to hold an almost religious faith in the truth of their own views, combined with an ability, worthy of a politician, to magnify minor points of difference into major disputes. We discover from Winklhofer, for example, that 'for more than a century after its composition, the formal architecture of Liszt's Sonata has eluded convincing explanation'[1] – until her own, of course, and so much for Newman, Longyear and the rest. Presumably until then all convincing performances of the Sonata, and the copies by Reubke and Liapunov, were achieved by serendipity.

In fact, when examined closely, some of the analytical arguments over the form of the Sonata are largely semantic – there is a measure of agreement over the function of the main structural divisions, if not over what to call them. On the latter point, the analysis of W. S. Newman has been most influential, particularly in his coining of the apt term 'double-function' form, a structure that can be considered both as one continuous movement and simultaneously as a composite of the movements of a multi-movement work.[2] In other words, the Sonata, though in one movement, exhibits elements of a first movement – slow movement – scherzo – finale structure. We shall see in more detail later how this is possible, but here it is enough to note that Newman was the first to elucidate in print this double-function view, although Dohnányi apparently taught something similar to his students in the Budapest Liszt Academy in the early years of this century.[3] Whatever their differences, Newman, Longyear and Winklhofer are at least agreed on one point: that the Sonata is not a programmatic work, and that as a result analysis of it can only proceed on purely musical terms. Liszt himself never dropped the slightest hint that the Sonata had a programme, but this is no problem, as several writers have been kind enough to supply one for him.

Programmatic interpretations

Programmatic approaches range from the vague to the breathtakingly specific. The vaguest of all was that of Peter Raabe, who contended that the Sonata was a musical autobiography, exploring the contradictory elements within Liszt himself, his triumphs and disappointments, his loves and his hates.[4] Whether this is true or not hardly seems to matter as it could apply to all of Liszt's mature music, and tells us nothing beyond the one thing that we already know for sure – that the Sonata was composed by Liszt and not a computer. Raabe's view was nevertheless given sterling support by the arranger of the music for the Hollywood film of Liszt's life, *Song Without End*, who adapted lyrical parts of the Sonata, scored for orchestra in the most lachrymose manner possible, to accompany various love affairs acted out in a rather uncomfortable fashion by Dirk Bogarde.

A second category of programmatic interpretation is the eschatological. Tibor Szász has advanced the revelation that the Sonata is an account of the struggle between God and Lucifer for the soul of man, based on the Bible and Milton's *Paradise Lost*.[5] Needless to say, the evidence for this is tangential in the extreme – one could as easily construct a programme for the Sonata based on Lamartine, or any other of Liszt's favourite authors. A similar programme has been suggested by Paul Merrick, who bolsters his view by noting that the Sonata's Grandioso theme has resemblances to the plainchant *Crux fidelis*, a favourite of Liszt that was later used, for example, in the symphonic poem *Hunnenschlacht* to represent Christianity.[6] With this proleptic resemblance Merrick constructs an amusing fantasy from which we learn, among other things, that 'the "slow movement" can represent only one thing: the redemption of Man after the Fall'. Such certitude would have been hotly contested by Bertrand Ott, who was as confident that the Sonata was a depiction of the Faust story as Merrick was that it was a religious tract.[7]

The Faust interpretation has been the most enduring of all programmatic descriptions. Cortot, in his Salabert edition of the Sonata, gives it as an accepted fact. Even the preface to the New Liszt Edition takes this as read, although it admits that the 'evidence' is based entirely on thematic similarities with the *Faust* Symphony. Lina Ramann, however, who wrote the first major biography of Liszt, and who questioned the composer closely on the origins of his works, stated categorically that the Sonata was not inspired by a programme.

Given Liszt's frequent panegyrics on programme music, it is not surprising that writers saw the Sonata as fair game. Liszt himself was quite capable of inventing a programme for a piece after the event, as in the case of *Les préludes*, in its original version an overture to Autran's *Les Quatre éléments* and nothing to do with Lamartine's eponymous poem. As we have seen, the titles of the *Transcendental* Studies made their appearance only in the 1851 version, with none but *Mazeppa* recomposed specifically to suit the programmatic description. Although Liszt attached titles and programmes to music conceived in other circumstances, there are no known instances of him deliberately hiding the source of his inspiration. The common ascription of the 'Hero and Leander' story, for example, to the second Ballade has no authentic basis. If the Sonata had really been based on, say, *Paradise Lost*, Liszt would hardly have regarded it as a shameful secret, but would have proclaimed it to the world. Ironically, the one dramatic association made by Liszt himself was that of the Sonata's theme 2 with the defiant mood of Beethoven's *Coriolan* Overture.[8] (I hesitate to mention this lest it precipitate a rash of articles asserting that the Sonata follows Heinrich von Collin's play *Coriolan* down to the minutest details.) Liszt suggested this to his pupil August Stradal during a lesson on the Sonata, and the context makes clear that it was intended as an aid in capturing the correct mood for performance of this theme. Many pianists construct programmes of their own for similar purposes.

The temptation to regard the Sonata as a counterpart to the *Faust* Symphony is at least understandable. As there is a *Dante* Symphony for orchestra and a *Dante* Sonata for piano, why not the same for Faust? Moreover, theme 3 of the Sonata (see page 35) bears a strong resemblance to a theme in the second movement of Alkan's *Grande sonate* of 1848, a movement entitled *Quasi Faust* (see Ex. 1).

This Alkan 'hammer-blow' theme is preceded on its first appearance by a motif in octaves, just as theme 3 in Liszt's Sonata is preceded by the octaves of theme 2. Later in the movement Alkan subjects his hammer-blow figure to a variety of lyrical transformations, again like Liszt. It would be convenient if we could prove that Liszt knew Alkan's *Grande sonate* by 1853, for these thematic similarities are certainly striking, and he was an admirer of Alkan's music. However, even if a connection between the Liszt and the Alkan sonatas were demonstrated, this would not be enough to show that the Sonata had a Faust programme.

The Sonata's theme 2 is indeed similar to one of the principal themes of Liszt's own *Faust* Symphony, but then it is also nearly identical with one of the *Grand Concert-solo* themes, for which no one has ever suggested a programme, and also to a theme in the symphonic poem *Ce qu'on entend sur*

Example 1   Alkan, *Quasi Faust*, bars 1–8

Example 2   Hummel, Sonata in F♯ minor, bars 1–4

la montagne. It is, in fact, one of Liszt's favourite melodic shapes. In the octave setting found in the Sonata, it probably has its inspiration in the opening octaves of Hummel's Sonata in F♯ minor (see Ex. 2).

To summarise this intentionally brief discussion, all the evidence tells us one thing: the Sonata is not a *roman à clef.*

Musical analyses

When we return from this land of programmatic make-believe to Newman's influential analysis of the Sonata, we are confronted with a minor problem. Newman illustrates his discussion with a chart mapping out the piece in

Table 1

Newman [Double function: four movements in one]	Longyear [Double function: three movements in one]	Winklhofer [One-movement sonata form]
Exposition (1–330?) [*first movement* in 'incomplete sonatina form']	Introduction (1–7) Exposition (8–178)	Exposition (1–204) comprising: *Thematic presentation* (1–17) Bridge (18–31) *Tonal presentation* (32–44) Transition (45–104) 2nd-subject area (105–19) Tonal deflection (120–40) Bridge (141–52) Cadential area (157–204)
Development (331–525): 1st part (331–459) [*Slow movement*] 2nd part (460–525) [*Scherzo*]	Development (179–459) [1–330 is *first movement*, 331–459 is a *slow movement*]	Development (205–452): 1st section (205–76) Transition (277–327) 2nd section (328–452) [Slow sub-movement in sonata form]
Recapitulation (525–681) [with coda forms *Finale* in 'incomplete sonatina' form]	Recapitulation (460–649) [with coda forms *Finale*]	Recapitulation (453–649): *Thematic presentation* comprising: Introduction (453–9) Fugato (460–508) Retransition (519–32) *Tonal presentation* (533–649)
Coda (682–760)	Coda (650–760)	Coda (650–760): 1st part (650–710) 2nd part (711–60)
(N.B. All bar numbers for Newman are approximate)	(N.B. This is according to Longyear's chart (p. 163). In the text he identifies bar 600 as the beginning of the 'proper "recapitulation"' (p.165))	

twenty-five-bar units, and neglects to give specific bar references to structural divisions.[9] This makes exact comparison with the analyses of Longyear and Winklhofer difficult, although the general outline of his approach is always clear.[10] Both Newman and Longyear agree that the Sonata can be considered either as a single movement in sonata form or as a multi-movement unit, with a slow movement and scherzo. They differ over whether the sections fall into four movements (Newman) or three (Longyear). Winklhofer remains aloof from this bone of contention, for she sees the Sonata only as one single movement, and rejects the double-function view as false. She admits that there is a 'slow sub-movement' in the centre, but refuses to identify the fugue with a scherzo. Table 1 attempts to summarise the three analyses for easier comparison.

Let us examine these contradictory positions. In the first place, all agree that the Sonata can be happily analysed as a single large-scale sonata form, however many arguments there might be over the details. On the 'double-function' question too, there may be less dissension than initially appears. Winklhofer herself is willing to grant the Andante sostenuto the status of a 'slow sub-movement in sonata form', and the difference between this and Longyear's 'slow movement' (*his* inverted commas) seems to me to be negligible. As Longyear also denies the 'scherzando' fugue an independent existence, including it in his 'Finale', we might regard his analysis as closer to Winklhofer's than she would like to admit. We have seen in the preceding chapter that other double-function structures can also be found in Liszt's output. *Ce qu'on entend sur la montagne* sports a profound Andante religioso slow section in the middle of the development which, as with the Sonata, is recapitulated in the tonic key in the coda. *Die Ideale* not only contains a funeral march slow section in the same place but follows it with a distinctly scherzo-like Allegretto mosso before the recapitulation. Winklhofer, of course, rejects any idea of a scherzo aspect to the Sonata fugue, and it has to be admitted that in some leaden performances the scherzando element is hard to discern. The fascination of the work is scarcely lessened by leaving the answer open: the fugue is a 'scherzo' if the performer chooses to project it as such, and the listener chooses to hear it as such.

The differences between Winklhofer and Newman are more acute. Longyear's three-movement division of the Sonata is consistent with his one-movement analysis – in other words, his 'first movement' is only a notional term that comprises the exposition and development of the Sonata as a whole, without the closing recapitulation that we would find in a true first movement. Newman's 'first movement' is the same part of the Sonata as Longyear's (bars 1-330), but here described as a self-contained unit in 'incomplete sonatina form', by which Newman means 'sonata form in which a simple retransition replaces the development section'. (In other words, it is what we have previously described as a 'slow-movement sonata form'.) What Longyear and Winklhofer consider as the beginning of the development, Newman hears as a recapitulation with its own mini-coda. In his view of the Sonata as a single movement, the development begins with the Andante sostenuto, which is consistent with his four-movement division, but irreconcilable with Longyear and Winklhofer. Bearing in mind the risk of simply adding another layer of contradictions to this confusing picture, let us now look at the Sonata in more detail.

Though we may be in territory unimagined by Reicha or Czerny, our most fruitful approach will be to begin analysis of the Sonata as a one-movement sonata form, leaving problems of double function to be elucidated later. By giving his work the simple title 'Sonata', Liszt ensured that the piece would be initially considered by musicians in relation to the familiar sonata archetype, the more so in that the overall key scheme conforms strictly to this archetype, unlike most of Liszt's sonata-form symphonic poems. The use of the relative major as the second tonal area, though a feature of some of Liszt's earlier sonata forms, and the dominant-major key for the central Andante sostenuto were deliberately conservative choices which focused attention on the more radical elements of the Sonata. Though Liszt's tonal goals may be conventional, his means of reaching them are dramatically new.

Thematically, the Sonata is concise but highly contrasted. The entire melodic fabric of the piece is constructed out of only five themes, the first three scarcely more than fragments in themselves, but capable of forming longer units by transformation or synthesis (see Ex. 3).

Theme 1 (Lento assai, bars 1–7) grows out of the slow syncopated repetition of the note G (muffled timpani-strokes, according to the *Liszt Pädagogium*, and not pizzicato strings as commonly played), the third repetition initiating a descending scale, firstly that of the Phrygian mode, secondly the Hungarian gypsy scale. The vacillation between the Phrygian (a scale most easily encountered by playing the white notes of the piano from E) and the gypsy scale (like our harmonic minor scale, but with a sharpened fourth) creates a pensive, brooding impression, enhancing the tentative groping of the repeated G's. The extra harmonic bite given by the tritone G–C♯ of the gypsy scale, further emphasised by the sustaining of the G octave in the right hand, increases the feeling of expectancy, fulfilled when a third repeat of the syncopated G's leads not to another scalar figure, but instead to theme 2 (Allegro energico, bars 8–13), a defiant motif in octaves outlining a diminished-seventh chord, the accented notes D (bar 10) and A (bar 12) creating harsh seventh suspensions against the implied harmony. This technique of a single line creating its own harmonic tensions and resolutions is ultimately derived from Bach's unaccompanied instrumental music. To see clearly how it works in this case, the reader need only play (or imagine) the diminished-seventh

Example 3   Liszt, Sonata in B minor, bars 1–17

chord A♯–C♯–E–G underneath the theme, and hear how the notes that Liszt has marked with an accent are dissonant to this basic harmony. Theme 2 reminded Liszt of the Coriolan of Beethoven's overture and Collin's play, haughtily announcing 'Why should I show my sorrows to them? I bear them within me, and proudly hide them away.'[11] Theme 3 (bars 13–17) was also specifically characterised by Liszt as a 'Hammerschlag' (hammer-blow), with obvious reference to its pounding single-note repetitions.[12]

These repetitions are a feature of all three themes. Theme 2 takes off from the repeated G of theme 1, now transformed into springing octaves (bar 8), and theme 3 begins by repeating the A♯ that ended theme 2, using it as part of the up-beat to its own repeated notes. Each new theme thus begins by pivoting on the note that completed the previous one, linking otherwise highly differentiated units in a continuous flow. The dissonant sevenths of theme 2 are also foreshadowed by the sevenths G–A♭ and G–A, outlined by the descending scales of theme 1, while the first phrase of theme 3 ends (bar 15) on an inversion of the same diminished-seventh chord that underpins theme 2. These links are particularly important, for the themes are designed otherwise to function as discrete *dramatis personae*, starkly recognisable even under their myriad future disguises. In this respect it is easy to see why so many commentators prefer to associate the themes with specific characters, Faust and Mephistopheles with themes 2 and 3, for example. Liszt's blatantly direct means of introducing his main thematic material seems to say 'here are my principal actors, let the play commence' almost as specifically as words themselves. Tonally speaking, however, the position is far less easily defined.

In the first of the wonderful subtleties that enrich this fascinating work, Liszt keeps the listener guessing even as he confirms thematic identities. The harmonic implications of theme 1 suggest C minor as the key, the repeated G's forming a dominant preparation. If, after the Lento assai, we were to play the fierce opening tune of *Orage*, from the Swiss volume of *Years of Pilgrimage*, this C minor melody would seem, tonally at any rate, completely appropriate. Instead we get theme 2, continuing the ambiguity by being based on a diminished seventh of no fixed tonal abode, although the possible resolution of the A♯–C♯–E–G chord on to a tonic chord of B minor hints that this may be the eventual destination. Theme 3 continues the tonal instability, both of its phrases ending on a diminished seventh.

In terms of phrase structure the situation is equally unstable, the typically Romantic four-bar phrase unit being nowhere to be seen. Theme 1 is composed of two three-bar phrases, a potential third phrase cut short by theme 2, a five-bar unit. Theme 3 is more regular, as befits hammer blows, dividing into two two-bar phrases. In view of the studied complexity of this opening page – the irregular phrasing, the tonal obscurity, the fragmentary nature of the themes – it is easy to understand why the piece struck some nineteenth-century listeners as completely incomprehensible. To audiences only gradually becoming used to the avant-garde music of Schumann and Chopin, whose sonatas at least had the decency to start with fairly regular melodies in the tonic key, the beginning of the Liszt Sonata must have appeared wilfully bizarre.

The *agitato* sequences that follow theme 3 seem finally to be leading up to some sort of tonic confirmation, and at bar 25 theme 2 duly reappears, but with its initial G harmonised by the totally unexpected chord of E♭ major in

Example 4   Liszt, Sonata in B minor, bars 32–9

first inversion. We must remember this harmonic shock, for it has important consequences both in the transition to the second-key area and in the recapitulation. B minor is eventually secured by a pounding *rinforzando* cadence (bars 30–2) using theme 3 to hammer home the tonic. The tonic material (bars 32–44) proves to be a contrapuntal combination of themes 2 and 3, aptly described by Brendel as the 'symphonic main idea' (using 'symphonic' in its original sense of 'sounding together').[13] For the first time in the Sonata, the music is now moving in regular phrases swinging between the tonic and subdominant chords of B minor. We have arrived at what in Czerny's scheme would be the first-subject area (see Ex. 4).

Liszt's delaying of tonic confirmation until bar 32, after the playing of the main themes, is the cause of the first disagreement among Newman, Longyear and Winklhofer that the reader will notice on the summarised analytical Table. For Newman the Sonata has no introduction, for Longyear it has a seven-bar introduction (i.e. the Lento assai), and for Winklhofer it has an exposition comprising separate thematic and tonal presentations. If, in normal terminology, anything before the first subject in the tonic is introductory, we might thus describe bars 1–31. Like most introductions, bars 1–31 function as a large-scale preparation for the tonic key, however ambiguous its initial intent might be. We may recall that the introduction to the first movement of Beethoven's First Symphony seemed radical to contemporaries on the grounds that it began with a cadence in the 'wrong key' (the subdominant). Liszt also begins out of key, but unlike Beethoven presents his main themes as well. The *Dante* Sonata uses exactly the same procedure.

The difficulty in accepting that an introduction might contain sections of different tempi partly accounts for Longyear's confining it to the Lento assai. For Liszt, however, multi-tempo introductions were commonplace (an idea he probably got from Berlioz, or from the last movement of Beethoven's Ninth Symphony). *Tasso*, as we have previously mentioned, has a tripartite Lento–Allegro energico–Lento assai introduction leading to a *slow* first subject in C minor (Adagio mesto). The *Faust* Symphony likewise has a tripartite introduction, as in the Sonata presenting many of the subsequent themes in their basic form. This idea of using the introduction as a thematic womb is peculiar to Liszt, and allows the hearer to follow subsequent transformations more easily.

Our view of the opening of the Sonata has consequences for our understanding of the recapitulation. If, with Longyear and Winklhofer, we hear the exposition as starting before the tonic confirmation at bar 32 then the recapitulation can logically begin before the return to the tonic key normally associated with recapitulations. Thus Winklhofer has a recapitulation paralleling the separate thematic and tonal presentations of her exposition. The return to theme 1 on F♯ at the end of the Andante sostenuto (bars 453–9) is the beginning of her thematic recapitulation, which is continued by the fugue thematically recapitulating themes 2 and 3 in extended form. Her tonal recapitulation begins of course at bar 533, where Liszt repeats bars 32–52 exactly. Longyear, true to his view of the exposition beginning with the Allegro energico at bar 8, hears the recapitulation starting with the fugue according to his analytical chart, although in his text he describes bar 600 (the return of the second-theme group) as the beginning of the 'proper recapitulation'. Longyear evidently does not regard the one place (bars 533–53) that Liszt repeats exactly music of the exposition as especially important, in fact he does not hear bars 32 and 533 as points of arrival at all, but rather as transitions. Newman, though hearing an exposition with no introduction at all, nevertheless places the recapitulation after the fugue at 525.

Recapitulations that begin in a key other than the tonic are certainly found in Classical practice. Mozart's little C major Sonata K.545 has a subdominant recapitulation of the first subject, a procedure that later was sometimes adopted by Schubert. Beethoven's *Coriolan* Overture, so highly admired by Liszt, also begins its recapitulation in the subdominant. Most commonly recapitulations that begin out of the tonic are intended as tonal sleights-of-hand, and are later corrected by the reappearance of the tonic. We could indeed describe bar 453 in Liszt's Sonata (the return to theme 1 on F♯) as the beginning of a tonally deceptive recapitulation. The repeated F♯'s of theme 1 imply the dominant of the tonic, B minor, which is then undershot by the move to B♭ minor, one semitone below the supposed goal. In the same way the initial presentation of theme 1 implied C minor instead of B minor. Alternatively, if we regard bars 1–31 as an introduction, then bar 453 is the return of the introduction in varied form as part of the development section, a procedure found in the first movement of the *Faust* Symphony and *Die Ideale*, among other Liszt works. There is no need to be dogmatic about either of these views, both of which are equally coherent.

However we describe it, we must recognise that Liszt's Sonata exhibits a binary division that should be taken into account in elucidating its formal structure, in other words the parallel between bars 1–17 and 453–69. The Reicha/Czerny sonata scheme recognises a binary division in combination with a tripartite plan, and we find this formal tension mirrored, though at different points in the structure, in the Liszt Sonata. Whether we describe bars 1–31 as an introduction, or as a separate non-tonic 'thematic' presentation, we are essentially describing the same thing, but our terminology here will affect our description of bars 453–532. What seems to me to be genuinely mistaken in Longyear is the under-emphasising of the tonic arrival at bars 32 and 533, a *rinforzando* cadence which was, according to Sauer's edition of the Sonata, further strengthened in Liszt's playing by additional octaves. These points represent to me the beginning of the exposition and recapitulation respectively, further confirmed by the exact repeat of bars 32–52 at 533–53. Tonally the fugue can only be part of the development section, although there is a strong feeling of varied introduction reprise at bars 453–532, described, if you prefer Winklhofer's terminology, as separation of thematic and tonal elements of the recapitulation. The procedure is similar to that used in the first movement of Beethoven's Sonata op. 10 no. 2, but massively expanded from a coy joke to a major structural effect.

In music there are rarely absolute truths, and it may well be that Longyear's view of the Sonata is more convincing for some listeners. From his writings it is obvious that he has devoted considerable thought to his analysis, and it would perhaps be possible to perform the piece in such a way that bars 32–52 are played as 'transition', though I confess I fail to see how.

Let us be thankful that at least by bar 45 of the Sonata all analysts are agreed that we are now in a transition section. Liszt begins a harmonic sequence, initially in two-bar phrases, but soon foreshortened at bars 51–4, where the sevenths so obvious in themes 1 and 2 take over in the right hand, leading to a *fortissimo* statement of theme 2 on a chord of B♭ major, enriched with canonic imitation. Given that theme 2 is based around a single chord, canonic manipulation is fairly simple. The distant resemblance, too, between theme 2 and various standard fugue themes – the Kyrie from Mozart's *Requiem*, or 'And with his stripes' from Handel's *Messiah*, both characterised by prominent falling diminished sevenths – should not be overlooked. The canonic sequence moves through the chords of B♭ major, G minor (marked by more intense dissonance in this position) and finally E♭ major *fff*. E♭ major has already been foreshadowed by the strikingly unexpected harmonisation in bar 25. What appears to be the triumphal goal of the procedure instead precipitates a dramatic tritonal collapse on to a diminished-seventh chord rooted on A in the bass (bar 81), the beginning of the long dominant preparation for the second-subject key of D, the traditional relative major.

As mentioned earlier, Liszt's procedure here – an excursion into flat-side keys to create a sense of distance between the tonic and the relative major – takes its basic inspiration from Hummel's F♯ minor Sonata. Parallels are even closer with the first movement of Chopin's Third Sonata, where the same tonal scheme is used: a tonic B minor, a fleeting passage through various distant keys culminating with E♭ major, and finally a descent on to the dominant of the true second-subject key, D major. When we also consider that the opening semiquaver figure of Chopin's main theme treated in sequence bears some family likeness to the descending triplets of Liszt's theme 2, we might hazard a guess that Liszt had Chopin's sonata in the back of his mind.

In pianistic style, however, they are quite different. Chopin rarely demands the formidable octave technique required in Liszt's bridge-passage. A laboured delivery of these octaves can be fatal to the musical intention of this section. None of the keys in Liszt's sequence is even remotely established. At bar 67, for example, we are *on* E♭ major rather than *in* it, and a dragging performance of bars 55–81, as well as giving the impression of an out-of-place octave study, can quite undermine the effect of the vertiginous tritone fall at bars 79–81 (*rinforzando!*).

The bass A on to which the music has landed turns out to be of melodic as well as harmonic interest, for it is soon heard to be one of the punctuated

Example 5   Liszt, Sonata in B minor, bars 105–13

repeated notes that begins theme 1, this time with a rising seventh (bars 83–4 etc.) before the scale figure in a linear synthesis of theme 1 and the inverted opening of theme 2. With an acute ear for instrumental colour, Liszt uses the lowest note on his (and our) piano to reinforce the dominant pedal. A sequence builds on theme 1 of gradually increasing intensity. The acerbic minor seconds created at bars 93–6 are particularly effective in sustaining tension, and are, of course, implied in the sevenths of theme 2 (the A–A♯ of bars 12–13), while the foreshortening of theme 1 from six-bar to two-bar phrases (93–100) leads inexorably and magnificently to theme 4 (Grandioso), the beginning of the second-key area of D major (see Ex. 5).

The first four bars of theme 4 constitute the so-called 'cross motif', based on the chant *Crux fidelis* and also used, for example, in the oratorio *St Elisabeth*. This has been the catalyst for many programmatic interpretations of the Sonata. Here it is enough to draw attention to the imaginative phrase structure of this splendid melody – two two-bar units then one five-bar phrase, in other words a solid beginning followed by a more impassioned, irregular extension.

41

The dissonant seventh (our old friend A–B♭ (A♯) again) of bar 110 is especially poignant, and even this far into the work it should be evident how much its harmonic and melodic character depends on this interval.

Having solidly established his second-key area and introduced a new theme, Liszt could, if following the standard pattern, proceed to close in D major and then either repeat the exposition or begin the development section. His sights, however, are set far more widely than this, and after a few bars (113–20) exchanging fragments of theme 4 he comes to rest on the diminished-seventh chord on A♯ outlined by theme 2, which theme he replays quietly at the opening pitch level, a sly allusion to the traditional exposition repeat that even Chopin felt unable to dispense with. At bar 124 he reinterprets the last A♯ of theme 2 enharmonically as B♭ and introduces a *dolce con grazia* transformation, hinting at the keys of F major and D minor before the now subdued hammer blows of theme 3, in a chromatic passage of exquisite beauty, remind us that we are still in D major. The lyrical elements of the second-subject group are about to make their appearance.

The basic function of this whole section (bars 120–52) is thus to form an emotional bridge between the two main units of the second subject group, gradually moving from the extrovert Grandioso to the more intimate material beginning at bar 153. Tonally, Liszt is careful to tread water and only suggest the possibility of moves to other keys. By beginning the section with a restatement of theme 2 at its original pitch, followed closely by theme 3, he alludes to the idea of an exposition repeat (if we are considering the exposition to begin at bar 8) or to a varied restatement of part of the introduction, before confirming that we are still in the second subject area at bar 153, with a *cantando espressivo* of italianate sensuality, a transformation of themes 3 *and* 2 (see Ex. 6).

Not only is the 'hammer blow' transfigured in augmentation, but theme 2 appears rapt as well (bars 161–2), its numinous quality underlined by a bass movement of tritones E–B♭, the greatest distance possible in the tonal system. Liszt wished this emphasized by a drop to *ppp una corda* for the B♭ chord.[14] The expressiveness of the transformation of theme 3 owes much to the harmony as well, the high point of the phrase underpinned by yearning seventh harmonies at bar 154. As the cantilena becomes more impassioned, rising to a climax at bar 168 (preceded by another anguished seventh harmony at bar 167), the regularity of the four-bar phrases is broken by three-bar units (bars 165–7, 168–70). A triplet decorated repeat of the opening of the cantilena leads into theme 2 again, retaining the E–B♭ harmonisation but conforming now to its original rhythmic shape, which facilitates a gradual increase in

Example 6   Liszt, Sonata in B minor, bars 153–62

rhythmic movement. We seem to be arriving at a development section as the sequences of theme 2 are foreshortened and a new *agitato* version of the cantilena arrives (bar 191). Suddenly movement is suspended. A trill hovers over an augmentation of theme 2, and we are plunged into the beginning of the main development section, Allegro energico (bar 205).

At this point, Newman believes a recapitulation begins rather than a development, to fit in with his idea of bars 1–328 as a self-contained 'incomplete sonatina form'. Longyear starts the development at bar 179, which is plausible enough as the music becomes significantly more restless here, while Winklhofer regards bar 205 as the true beginning of the development. The difference between the latter two opinions is simply a reflection of Liszt's careful dovetailing of sections, but Newman's view is more difficult to accommodate. Bars 205–330 have all the characteristics we would normally attribute to development sections: tonal instability, thematic fragmentation and sequential treatment of themes. To be sure, Liszt uses all these techniques at other points in the Sonata, but the one thing that might allow us to call bars 205–330 a recapitulation – a firm return to the tonic – is lacking. There are hasty glances towards the tonic at bars 213 and 245, which are immediately drawn into other areas in sequential continuations. When theme 2 returns in the double octaves that marked its first appearance (bar 286) it is at a pitch level that implies F minor not B minor, and it leads into two *pesante* transformations of theme 4 juxtaposed with impassioned recitatives based on a retrograde version of theme 2. The turmoil slowly settles down at bars 319–30, with a pedal on B (theme 3 in the bass in combination with an augmented theme 2) pointing towards a possible cadence in E.

It appears to me that the only point in this developmental flux that one might vaguely imagine to be recapitulatory – albeit 'false' – is theme 2 in double octaves from bar 286 prefaced by theme 1 beginning on G. Even here the listener would be quickly disabused of the notion within a few bars. A possible false recapitulation at bar 275 or 286 nevertheless does not tally with Newman's notion of the whole of bars 205–330 as recapitulatory, and I fail to see the basis for his opinion. Had Liszt been composing a sonata form of normal length, however, bar 275 would have been the obvious point to begin the 'true' recapitulation.

Any expectation of a move to E after the pedal on B is thwarted by the deflection of the music into F♯ major. It is a feature of Liszt's overall tonal strategy in the Sonata that dominant preparations should only reach their obvious goal for the arrival of the tonic and second-subject keys. The Andante sostenuto reaches F♯ by means of a tonal side slip, and commences with the last new melody of the Sonata: theme 5 (bars 331–46), related in its second part (bars 339–40) to theme 3, and also sporting the typical inverted-seventh leap that makes a distant connection with theme 2 (see Ex. 7).

The constant return to one repeated note (C♯) at bars 335–8 may remind us of the repeated notes beginning theme 3, especially as Liszt now brings back the cantilena version of theme 3 in A (bar 349), allowing us to hear the same C♯'s in a different context.

The Andante sostenuto is itself a miniature sonata form. The return of the cantilena theme 3 in A is its brief second subject. The central, development, section returns initially to F♯ to present the Grandioso theme 4, with a continuation that harks back to theme 2 and the developmental recitatives at bars 301 and 306. The cunning of the harmonic sideslip that began the Andante becomes more apparent when Liszt uses it again (bars 393–5) to re-establish F♯ major for the recapitulation of theme 5. The cantilena theme 3 duly returns in the F♯ tonic (bar 433), but not before a hushed and intensely

Example 7   Liszt, Sonata in B minor, bars 331–40

moving harmonic interlude (bars 415–33) muses over various distant chords to the descending scales of theme 1.

When theme 1 resurfaces in the bass on F♯ (bar 413) we might confidently expect the recapitulation in B minor for which the Andante sostenuto has been such a huge dominant preparation. Instead Liszt reads F♯ as G♭ and launches into a fugal Allegro energico that is either development or part of a non-tonic recapitulation, or a scherzo, or not, depending on your reaction to this stroke of genius. Though much of the material of the Sonata has been treated contrapuntally before, Liszt here writes a three-voice fugal exposition with a subject formed from themes 2 and 3, in B♭ minor, a semitone below the anticipated key. Fugal development sections themselves are not unusual, Beethoven's op. 101 and 106 sonatas contain famous examples, but to begin one after an already extensive development, including an Andante movement, was unprecedented.

The fugue's chattering, sardonic counterpoint gradually transforms itself in masterly fashion into a more homophonic texture, a process initiated by the combination of theme 2, articulated in chords, with theme 3 (bars 502–8). A middle voice, also sounding theme 3, produces a stretto between the two lower parts. The palpable increase in intensity here is fostered by this superimposition of one half of the fugue subject (theme 2) over the other (theme 3), creating a two-bar microcosm. As well as swelling the sheer volume of sound, the new chordal setting of theme 2 facilitates the transition into the heavier keyboard textures of the true recapitulation. At bar 509 the theme 2 chords take on a more agitated dotted rhythm while the left hand forsakes theme 3 to take up theme 2 – but in inversion. The combination of theme 2 with its own inversion is Liszt's last contrapuntal gambit, and it appears for a moment that he may be about to begin another fugal exposition, this time using the inversion of theme 2, when the left hand gives the traditional fugal answer in octaves, a fourth below (bars 513–18). The octaves, however, harbingers of recapitulation, are taken up in the right hand in outline of theme 2, the harmony veering towards E minor. As in the exposition (bars 22–6) the suggestion of E minor is merely a mirage to give force to the *fortissimo* E♭ chord that wrenches the music around, in a passage that parallels the initial confirmation of B minor, but expanded and intensified to a dissonant seventh climax at bar 529. Liszt now repeats exactly the cadence in B minor and the subsequent 'symphonic main idea'.

In a typical sonata we should now expect the recomposition of the transition passage to the second group, in order to retain the tonic key. Our expectations are not disappointed, but rather surpassed by the fertility of Liszt's invention. At bar 554 the chromatic flux that introduced the B♭–G minor–E♭ sequences of theme 2 (bars 55–79) takes a new turn. We land on a chord of E♭ again, but without the intervening sequence. This chord of E♭ now accompanies theme 1 (bars 555–60) to begin a secondary development, which, however, serves to reaffirm the tonic of B rather than move away from it. The E♭ chord retains its first-inversion bass of G, but the upper voices soon move on to B and E♮, and theme 1 is repeated again. The G bass falls to F♯, the dominant of B, and themes 2 and 1 alternate in different registers of the keyboard. The various shapes taken by the two themes can do nothing to halt the ineluctable pull towards B, its dominant pedal anchored in the bass. A frantic *stringendo* on theme 2 (bars 582–94) and a last violent sneer from theme 3 are answered by the Grandioso theme 4, luminously brought home to the tonic major. (I feel compelled to admit, in blatant contradiction to everything I have written about the Sonata and programmaticism, that when playing this page I cannot avoid thinking of the final defeat of Mephistopheles and the redemption of Faust.) The lyrical part of the second subject follows hard on the heels of theme 4, wisely shorn of the intervening transition, but also demonstrating its necessity in the first place, for the juxtaposition of the two parts of the second subject would surely have seemed surprisingly abrupt in the exposition.

Parallels now appear with the development, for the cantilena flows into a *stretta* passage similar to bars 255–76 but starting a minor third lower with a chord of E♭ (spelt enharmonically as D♯). We will recall that this passage in the development led into the Sonata's initial false recapitulation – theme 1 descending from G (bars 277–86) followed by theme 2 suggesting the 'wrong' key of F minor. At bar 673 we duly hear theme 1 in the same position again, but played Presto with its initial G immediately contradicted by G♯ – simultaneously the beginning of the coda and a reworking of the false recapitulation, now transformed in the home key. Theme 1 increases in momentum to open the gates for a jubilant Prestissimo variant of theme 2, crowned eventually by the triumphal arrival of theme 4, *fff* in B major. We are now surely on the threshold of a clamorous final cadence, but Liszt, after setting the entire keyboard ringing with the dominant seventh of B, suddenly breaks off.

A silence prefaces a reminiscence of the Andante sostenuto in the tonic, its final cadence strangely interrupted (bars 728–9). The bass has indeed landed on B, but the upper parts outline the diminished-seventh chord of theme 2, the harmony that prepared the way for the Andante's first appearance (bars 328–330). The Andante reminiscence seems to be going into reverse as the bass intones the sinister chatter of theme 3 on B, while the upper parts grope tentatively at a series of mystic chords, arriving at theme 2 with bar 737, shorn of all energy, reduced to a forlorn monody. A weak cadence on a chord of B major is darkened twice by a reminder of the dissonant G with which the Sonata began. Theme 1, on B, snakes down deep in the bass ending on an accented C♮. As if on upper woodwind, three chords are floated above – A minor, F major ⁶₃, B major ⁶₄. The written description is prosaic; the effect is the most inspired tritone cadence ever composed. In an echo of the Sonata's inchoate beginning, the closing B major chord is belatedly given its true bass, almost as an afterthought, with a stroke of the lowest B on the keyboard.

This narrative account of the Sonata has, I hope, explained how its evident formal coherence can nevertheless generate considerable analytical dissension. The ambiguity is an essential part of its richness and originality. In this it is a true successor not only to the late sonatas of Beethoven, but also to the piece for which it was reciprocally dedicated, Schumann's *Fantasy*. If the sonata archetype only hovers in the background of the first movement of Schumann's *Fantasy*, Liszt's Sonata deliberately conforms to the basics of the Reicha/ Czerny scheme, massively expanding its range but remaining recognisably a sonata form.

In setting himself this challenge Liszt looked for new ways to accommodate the tonal radicalism of his sonata-form symphonic poems. Many of these orchestral works had been completed in early versions before the composition of the Sonata, and in them we have seen that Liszt found the use of the major third above the tonic especially congenial for second-subject areas, particularly in minor keys. A similar approach in the Sonata would place the second-subject group in E♭ major, and it is no coincidence that E♭ acts as a sort of 'Banquo's ghost' in the Sonata, turning up in the most unexpected places. In fact the goal of the bridge passage between first- and second-subject areas seems for sometime to be E♭ major, tonally deflected at the last minute towards D in a sudden dramatic peripeteia.

Though discussion of Liszt's use of E♭ might superficially appear to be only concerned with arcane questions of tonal areas in sonata forms, the effect of his approach is so immediate and vivid – even to listeners with no academic knowledge of music – that it constantly suggests programmatic analogues. In other words, Liszt's ultimate aim was always direct emotional communication. The opposite approach can be seen in so much of the music of his lesser contemporaries. Ironically, the affective impact of Liszt's music was so real that for decades some musicians could scarcely believe that his larger pieces were in any recognisable form at all, and to this day we come across nonsense about Liszt's lack of interest in sonata form. No Romantic composer was more aware than Liszt of the sonata tradition and its relevance to the formal structure of his larger works. If this has taken a long time to be recognised, it is because thoughtless repetition of Identikit forms was anathema to Liszt. His sonata forms are not still-born Reicha/Czerny clones.

4

Text and texture

Given Liszt's experience in composing sonata forms prior to 1853, we should, perhaps, not be too surprised that the Sonata manuscript shows the overall structure was clear in his mind at an early stage (assuming we do not find a bundle of hitherto unknown sketches in some dusty Weimar attic). We might, however, allow ourselves some astonishment at the degree of confidence shown in the structural organisation of the basic layer of the manuscript. Many of the symphonic poems went through several complete versions before publication, the revisions sometimes drastically altering the formal design. With the Sonata there seemed to have been relatively little doubt or hesitation over even the most complex element of its structure: the accommodation within a sonata form of a slow section and fugal 'scherzo'. The fugue, in particular, which has been the source of so much disagreement among analysts, was evidently integral to the original conception. The slow section, an afterthought as far as the *Grand Concert-solo* was concerned, was again part of the initial inspiration. In its basic design the tonal and formal conservatism of some elements of the Sonata are offset by what might be called 'structural puns' that relate to the binary–ternary dichotomy of the traditional scheme. The most obvious of these is the function of the fugue, heard as a development, recapitulation or even 'scherzo' movement, depending on the interpretation of what has gone before. These separate views are not necessarily contradictions. The fugue can perform each of these functions in the structure, although our conception of the Sonata as a whole will differ accordingly. The greatness of the work lies in its ability to support varied analyses, facilitated by its series of deceptive recapitulations and tonal evasions. Far from being evidence of a free or loose approach to form, this richness of meaning arises from Liszt's total compositional control, nowhere more striking than in his manipulation of phrasing and use of sequential repetition. The chief tonal anchors of the structure (first- and second-subject areas, for example) display a regularity of phrase length deliberately absent from most of the piece. This is all the more remarkable given that so many of Liszt's contemporaries were unable to avoid the rut of a tediously unbroken four-bar phrase structure.

Sequential repetition, too, is for Liszt an aid to structural articulation, not an automatic means of padding out undernourished inspiration. At bar 221, for example, the gradual foreshortening of the sequence precipitates the music up to bar 232, a cataclysm that is the harbinger of the transformation of theme 2 beginning a few bars later. In his protean treatment of phrasing and sequence, Liszt showed that he learned more from Beethoven than most of his Romantic contemporaries.

Also Beethovenian is the welding of short thematic units into larger paragraphs. Liszt's first three themes in the Sonata are hardly more than fragments, yet most of the piece consists of their combination or extension. Although overtly contrasted, these three themes show some interrelation-ships, as previously described. It would be a mistake to make too much of this, for Liszt's themes are fashioned out of the basic building blocks of music in such a way that relationships would be very difficult to avoid. Of more importance is the harmonic reliance on the interval of the seventh, which colours so much of the Sonata that it must be regarded as the most characteristically expressive feature of its harmony.

The thematic working of Liszt's music, important as it is, has often attracted more than its fair share of attention. Even students to whom Liszt is merely a synonym for 'excessively difficult piano music' seem to remember that he invented thematic transformation. They can be forgiven for cherishing this nugget of misinformation, for many of the most influential writers on Liszt in English – for example Humphrey Searle – have perpetuated it. The result is that Liszt's music is regularly scoured for thematic transformation, and once the melodies and their variations are identified, little more appears to be of interest. The symphonic poem *Les préludes* is one of the most conspicuous victims of this approach. Few discussions of it proceed much beyond the transformations of the little melodic tag with which it begins.

Liszt himself never claimed any inventor's rights over thematic transforma-tion. He knew that melodic variation was as old as the hills. He knew too that the basis of his own transformation technique had been laid down by Beethoven, Schubert and Berlioz. We have already mentioned (in Chapter 2) the thematic transformations in Beethoven's Ninth Symphony and Schubert's *Wanderer* Fantasy. Berlioz was a no less potent influence. The *ne plus ultra* of Liszt's use of thematic transformation is the Mephistopheles movement of the *Faust* Symphony, a sardonic metamorphosis of the Faust movement. Mephistopheles begins with a passage so similar to the opening of the last movement of Berlioz's *Symphonie fantastique* (the Witches' Sabbath) that an intentional allusion can scarcely be doubted, especially as Berlioz's own macabre transformation of his *idée fixe* theme is of identical parodistic effect to Liszt's Mephistopheles. Liszt's claim to originality in the *Faust* Symphony lies in the scale of his use of thematic transformation – to write an entire movement as a variation of another, particularly one as extended and complex as the Faust movement, was unprecedented.

The transformations in the *Faust* Symphony have a dramatic as well as a musical purpose, similar to Wagner's use of Leitmotifs in his later operas. In other words, Liszt's themes function as characters in a drama, and we can experience their variation as the vicissitudes of their lives. Programmatic interpretations of the Liszt Sonata often adopt a similar approach, with the Sonata's most striking transformation – the hammer-blow theme turned into the second-subject cantilena – interpreted in dramatic terms. Liszt, though never condoning programmatic interpretations of the Sonata, was particularly glad that its first reviewer, Louis Köhler, had noticed this thematic transformation, which is certainly one of his most effective. He was also, as it happens, pleased with the transformation of the slow-section theme of the First Piano Concerto into a rumbustious march, which has unfortunately garnered less approbation from critics. Most vilified of all has been the march transformation in the Second Concerto, usually condemned with a disgust otherwise reserved for capital crimes. Yet Liszt was proud of both these works, and commented regarding the transformations in the First Concerto that 'this kind of *binding together* [Liszt's italics] and rounding off a whole piece at its close is somewhat my own, but it is quite maintained and justified from the stand point of musical form'.[1]

If Liszt was indeed aware that thematic transformation was not unique to his works, then how are we to justify this claim to originality? Firstly, we come to questions of scale. Thematic transformation plays such a large part in Liszt's output that it constitutes a central feature of his style. Secondly, the most remarkable of Liszt's transformations are of a type we find least in other composers (outside variation sets): the metamorphosis of one extended melody into another of different character. The reason that the *idée fixe* transformation from the *Symphonie fantastique* seems so Lisztian is that it is a variation of precisely this type. Ironically, *Les préludes* is a bad example for this more typical sort of Lisztian transformation, because most of its thematic working is based on the elaboration of one three-note fragment in a manner found in many composer's works. The transformation of the long lyrical melody from the slow movement of the First Concerto is very different, and in effect forms a complete varied recapitulation of the slow section in the tonic key of E♭. This is what Liszt meant when he wrote of 'binding together' the piece by this means.

The chief objection to the thematic transformations in the two concerti has always been that they consist of changing a winsome, lyrical melody into a blatantly vulgar one, without even the excuse of parody that Liszt had in Mephistopheles. On the other hand, the transformation in the Sonata of an aggressive, biting figure into a soulful cantabile has usually been praised. It is tempting to believe that had the transformations in the concerti gone in the opposite direction, they would not have been found so tasteless. Had Liszt started with the march version, then modified it for a slow movement, this might have been seen as 'sensitive', whereas the other approach is branded 'crude'. Questions of taste such as these can only be answered separately by each individual listener, but they are often raised when Liszt's music is criticised, and stem largely from Liszt's eclectic enjoyment of many different styles of music. In no other Romantic composer, with the possible exception of Meyerbeer, is there such a range of differing stylistic elements – from Germanic chromaticism and thematic development to italianate lyricism, taking in elements from French Grand Opera and Hungarian gypsy music along the way. That Liszt was able to weld these into a distinctive personal style was one of his most remarkable achievements.

The synthesis is nowhere more effective than in the B minor Sonata. If the cantilena second subject appears italianate, albeit married to distinctly un-Italian chromatic harmony, then the majestic repeated chords of the Grandioso theme recall no less the world of the French Grand Opera chorus – compare the 'Blessing of the Daggers' scene from *Les Huguenots* – transfigured by a melody of vastly greater nobility. (Similar writing can be found in *Invocation* from *Harmonies poétiques et religieuses*.) The Sonata's opening 'gypsy' scale proclaims Liszt's Hungarian influences, as does the distinctly Hungarian turn of phrase at bar 375, which reminds us of William Mason's statement that Liszt was always adding Hungarian ornamental turns when performing.

The Sonata's keyboard style is uniquely Liszt's in its contrast of tessitura and texture. Unlike the music of Brahms, which mostly unfolds in block writing around the centre of the keyboard, Liszt's music ranges through all areas of the instrument and displays an acute ear for piano sonority. This feeling for tonal colour is not some sort of meretricious overlay on top of the music, but is part of the music itself. The thud of the lowest note on the keyboard adds significantly to the effect of the dominant-pedal preparation for the Grandioso second subject, while the contrast between registers at the very end of the piece is essential to its meaning – the B major resolution in the high treble arriving long before that of the bass. For reasons that seem to stem from some sort of puritan urge to cut off potential sources of pleasure, Liszt's very command of the keyboard has sometimes resulted in criticism of his music as 'superficial brilliance'. Liszt's range is far greater than that, but when brilliance is required he is eminently capable of producing it.

Most imaginative of all is Liszt's protean variety of keyboard figuration, which so often in the Sonata is derived from the main thematic shapes. Theme 2 is especially promising in this regard, its outline snaking around a diminished-seventh chord. Played in continuous semiquavers, theme 2 automatically turns itself into memorable and – just as important – easily playable figuration. Throughout the work, runs, which in other contexts might seem merely glittering digital pyrotechnics, prove to be integral parts of the motivic texture. The *stringendo* figuration at bars 232–6, for example, is at once the climax of the preceding developmental passage and a continuation of its process of foreshortening, squeezing the theme into rapid semiquavers around its basic diminished-seventh chord. Elsewhere the figuration forms a Schumannesque anticipation of the principal line (bars 179– 90), or is formed from its inversion (bars 161–2, see Ex. 6, p. 43) This gives the pianist a myriad of opportunities to subtly underline inner parts and draw attention to the music's tight thematic logic, which is nowhere more complex than in the 'symphonic' main idea of the first-subject group (bars 32–9, see Ex. 4, p. 37).

This first-group material might act as a microcosm for Liszt's thematic development of passage work. If we turn back to Example 4 we can see that the combination of themes 2 and 3 is accompanied by continuous passage work formed from the fragmentation of the themes themselves. At bars 32–3 the complete right-hand melody starting D–E♯–F♯–A is anticipated in the semiquavers of the left, which flows directly into a statement of theme 3. The right hand takes over the thematic semiquavers while the left is occupied with the theme 3 quavers, and the result is a motivic crucible of the two themes. Steady semiquaver motion is maintained by alternation between the hands, and the constant reversal of the relative positions of melody and accompaniment ensures textural variety. On top of all this, the close juxtaposition of themes 2 and 3, following each other bar after bar, forces the listener's attention to the fact that the shape of the first three notes of theme 2 (D–E♯–F♯) is

Example 8   Liszt, Sonata in B minor, manuscript, bars 600–4, original version

inverted in the last three of theme 3 (C♯–G–F♯). By bar 40, the marriage of the two themes has become so complex that the descending diminished-seventh semiquavers of theme 2 has acquired the triplet upbeat that originally belonged to theme 3, even though the theme itself has now vanished.

This prose description may seem – indeed is – a pedantic and laboured peroration of some tremendously exciting music, made more redundant by the fact that Liszt's procedure here is aurally quickly grasped. It is necessary only to emphasise Liszt's outstanding talent for combining taut musical texture with pianistic brilliance. Even if the thematic intricacies are not fully understood – although surely after a few hearings they can hardly fail to be – the keyboard writing is overwhelmingly thrilling.

The care Liszt took over the pianistic setting of his music is immediately evident from the manuscript of the Sonata. The Lento opening, originally written an octave higher than the final version, was moved into the lower register to enhance its lugubrious, pensive atmosphere, and to increase the contrast with the higher-register octaves of theme 2 that follow. A similar concern was shown over accompaniment figuration. Even in the rare places where the subsidiary voices do little more than fill out the harmony, Liszt frequently took pains to consider variants before settling on the final version. The recapitulation of theme 4 (bars 600–4) was originally accompanied by triplet chords, eventually rejected, no doubt, because of their inappropriately jaunty rhythm (see Ex. 8).

After replacing the triplets with the version we have today, Liszt had the further idea of adding theme 2 in the bass, creating a contrapuntal combination similar to that of the 'symphonic main idea' (see Ex. 9). This was eventually scored out at the very last stage of the compositional process, when he was adding dynamics and making final corrections, perhaps because the height-ened dissonance would undermine the sense of harmonic resolution on to B major. Nevertheless, the combination works so well that I for one harbour

Example 9   Liszt, Sonata in B minor, manuscript, bars 600–4, second version

pangs of regret at its demise (and have sometimes been tempted to play it anyway).

There can, however, be little argument that the major manuscript revisions improved the Sonata immensely. Though the overall outline of the work was indeed clear in Liszt's mind at an early stage, some sections required fairly extensive redrafting, namely the transition to the Andante sostenuto, the central part of the Andante itself, and the coda. Lesser, but still important, revisions were made to bars 18–32 – the lead up to the 'symphonic main idea' and confirmation of B minor as the tonal centre – and to the Più mosso of the recapitulation (bars 555–99). Some of these revisions were first mentioned by José Vianna da Motta in the preface to the Franz-Liszt-Stiftung edition, and they are all discussed extensively, along with others, by Winklhofer in her book.

It is interesting to note that at bar 277–96, the hint of a false recapitulation was initially far less obvious, the descending scales of theme 1 first leading into another developmental treatment of themes 2 and 3, rather than the return in double octaves of theme 2 that reminds us of its first appearance. The draft of this version eventually falters inconclusively after three repetitions of theme 2, each a third higher than the one before. It is probably not just hindsight that makes this transition seem weak and over-reliant on diminished-seventh harmonies. A second version omitted theme 2 altogether, in favour of a portentous augmentation of theme 1, leading straight into the newly composed, familiar, *pesante* recitative at bar 297. This unfortunately fatally undermines the impact of the dramatic augmentation of theme 4 by having drastically slowed down the musical motion a good eight bars before, in a rhythmic transition as abrupt as it is premature. Finally, Liszt retained the augmented theme 4 but decided upon the far more flexible and sophisticated 'false reprise' repeat of theme 2, continued sequentially in heavy octaves as a join.

The original Andante sostenuto, in a mini sonata form like the final version, had a much more extensive development section, followed by a less climactic return of the Andante main theme. The musical weight was thus firmly on the central section, which contained additional material based on the alternation of an augmented theme 4 with theme 3. The main theme of the Andante then sneaked back in a quiet and rather lame fashion, completely unlike the glorious *fff* paean we know today. Most distressing of all, the wonderful harmonic meditation of bars 415–33 is nowhere to be found. Liszt made room for it (he had evidently decided on an optimum length for the Andante as a whole) by omitting the latter part of the development. In doing so he remodelled the climax structure so that it centred around the beginning of the recapitulation. It is a thought-provoking observation that the Andante's greatest gain in the final version is the one passage (bars 415–33) where the music is, harmonically at least, treading water. Relaxation of tension is as necessary in some places in a work of this scale as constant forward motion is in others.

Of the greatest importance of all was the rewriting of the coda. Until the very last compositional stage the Sonata ended soon after the apotheosis of theme 4 (bars 700–10) with a forceful presentation of theme 1 prefacing a loud, extrovert cadence in B major.

Liszt had even given this ending its final marks for dynamics and articulation before having second thoughts and replacing it with the wonderful, mystic conclusion that stands in the score. An identical process took place with the Ballade in B minor. The original virtuoso coda was substituted at the proof stage for a more restrained and sophisticated version, to the immense improvement of the piece as a whole. For the *Dante* Symphony Liszt published alternative codas, though the preface to Stradal's piano arrangement informs us that in later life Liszt considered the quiet ending to be the most appropriate. The alternative codas to the song 'The Three Gypsies' sport a significant footnote to the effect that though the loud ending might be preferred for public performance, the other will appeal more to musicians. There is no reason why a quiet conclusion should be inherently preferable – the magnificent coda to the *Vallée d'Obermann* is a case in point – but with the Sonata there can be no doubt that the new ending improved the work substantially. Not only does the second coda contain one of the most inspired final cadences in the entire keyboard literature (the original was the hackneyed

Example 10   Liszt, Sonata in B minor, manuscript, original coda

dominant–tonic) but it also integrates the Andante sostenuto into the recapitulation, making it a true summation of the piece.

From manuscript to printed text

Given Liszt's meticulous care over every aspect of the Sonata's composition – his indefatigable redrafting of unsatisfactory sections, careful working-out of keyboard figuration and, finally, his copious and detailed manuscript markings for dynamics, phrasing and articulation – one might safely assume that he would have taken similar pains to ensure that published editions were as accurate as possible. Like many racing certainties, this falls at the first hurdle, namely the original Breitkopf und Härtel edition of 1854. The edition, along with a reprint around 1880, was the only one to appear during Liszt's lifetime, and it proves to be in many ways a less satisfactory source than the autograph manuscript, which gives more detailed performance information. Liszt joked that he was a good proof-reader for all music apart from his own, and, considering the other pressing demands on his time in Weimar from 1853–4, it is probable that he did not have much time to devote to checking the Sonata. Moreover, the work's first champions were mostly Liszt's own students, who could rely on the composer himself to make his intentions clear to them.

It is from the account of one of these students – Karl Klindworth – that one of the most puzzling problems arises, though in this case the manuscript and published edition are at one. In his preface to the Franz-Liszt-Stiftung edition, José Vianna da Motta, himself a Liszt pupil, claimed that Klindworth had been told by Liszt to alter the melody-note D♯ to D♮ in bars 738 and 740. This is no paltry change, for the D♮ gives the melody a completely different, depressive, quality and totally changes the character of this section. Klindworth apparently also argued that the D♮ found a logical continuation in the C♯♯ of bar 743, which is only resolved on to D♯ at 744. If the D♯ had already been anticipated at 738 and 740, this enharmonic resolution would lose its power. Da Motta sums up: 'Played with the minor suspended note D ... the chord contains a twinge of bygone sorrow; with D♯ it seems considerably more peaceful, cooler. It is quite conceivable that the master wanted to change the D♯ to D later, after the publication of the Sonata. However, I have not yet been able to find a reliable document.' Da Motta duly printed D♯ in the text, as do all editions that I have seen. The manuscript clearly has D♯.

It is difficult to believe that Klindworth either mistook or made up the story about D♯. There are several problems with doubtful accidentals in the Sonata, but only one other (discussed below) is musically significant or even particularly noticeable in performance. If the reader plays the different versions of bars 737–41 one after another, s/he will hear that a change to D♮ is not something easily forgotten. What is also certain is that by the time August Stradal played the Sonata to Liszt (in the 1870s), the story about the D♮ was already well established, for Ramann in the *Liszt Pädagogium*, working from notes taken by Stradal, says that the D♯ must not be changed. This appears to represent Liszt's final decision, and if he did indeed instruct Klindworth to play D♮, then it can only have been a short-lived change of mind soon after the Sonata's publication. Da Motta described Ramann's prohibition of the D♮ as 'without foundation', although there seems to be no reason to doubt her role as an honest reporter in the *Pädagogium*. Liszt's pupil, Emil von Sauer, who heard Arthur Friedheim perform the Sonata in the composer's presence, prints D♯ without comment in his Peters edition, although he makes two other changes to the text as 'according to Liszt's intentions'. In my opinion, the D♮ reading is much inferior to the D♯, casting an unwanted gloom over the atmosphere of fragile expectancy that seems appropriate. I have yet to hear any performance in which D♮ was played.

In bar 301, on the contrary, different readings of the third left-hand chord are often heard. Since neither in the autograph nor in the first edition did Liszt cancel the sharp before the E implied by the second chord, the third chord should strictly speaking read A♯–E♯–G♯. The main problem with this is that it sounds terrible. The analogous passage at bar 306 clearly has a diminished-seventh chord at this point, and some pianists play the same chord in 301 adopting the reading A♯–E–G. The other viable solution is the more astringent A♯–E–G♯, which might seem preferable in the context, and is the reading adopted by the New Liszt Edition, among others.

Occasionally, Liszt's use of abbreviation to indicate his intentions has caused confusion. The strangely unmusical accents over the first note of every bar in the right hand from bars 277 to 285 that we find in the first edition, and also in Joseffy's Schirmer edition, result from Liszt writing out the first bar of each harmonic change fully, and then writing repeat signs for the next two bars. In the Breitkopf und Härtel edition, the repeat signs were taken to include the initial accent, producing a crude emphasis every bar rather than every three bars at the significant changes of chord. Most editors from Da Motta onwards realised that Liszt's intentions were perverted here.

More complicated is the distinction between a bass note transposed down an octave (indicated by Liszt as '8 bassa') and a bass note doubled in the lower octave (indicated by placing '8' under the note). The New Liszt Edition tries to avoid confusion by writing the doubled octaves out in full. Other editions are less reliable and a variety of interpretations are found, especially for the exposition transition passage to the Grandioso (bars 82–8), where the low A is sometimes indicated singly (Sauer's edition) and sometimes doubled at the octave (Da Motta, Joseffy, New Liszt Edition). It is clear that Liszt intended a doubled octave here, and also in the very last bar of the piece.

Those wishing to explore more fully the differences between the manuscript and the printed editions should consult the critical notes of the Henle and New Liszt Editions, and Longyear's article 'The Text of Liszt's B Minor Sonata'. Even if the original had been slavishly faithful to the manuscript, it would still have represented an inadequate guide to some aspects of performance. Indications as to the use of the sustaining pedal are scanty in the extreme, appearing only at bars 105–10 (the Grandioso tune) and 555-68 (the recomposed bridge passage in the recapitulation). In both places the function of the sustaining pedal is to increase the volume as well as to aid the legato. At bars 105–10 the fact that the bass octaves are written only as quavers might, I suppose, lead an exceptionally stupid player to cut them off, had the pedal not been indicated. Bars 555–68 could indeed be played without pedal, although the resulting dry, motoric repeated chords sound more like Stravinsky than Liszt. There are, however, hundreds of other places that Liszt could have indicated the sustaining pedal – a performance without copious pedal is quite inconceivable. This is not mere prejudice – try playing the cantando second subject without pedal. Why, then, was Liszt so miserly with his markings?

Liszt's approach to pedal indications was always inconsistent. In the G minor study of the *Grandes études* (later titled *Vision*) he marks no pedal until nearly half way through the piece, despite the fact that the first page is to be played with the left hand alone – quite impossible without constant pedal. When the pedal is actually indicated, at the climactic turn to G minor, it seems to be there to underscore the increased volume required. A bar after that, specific pedal markings disappear. This is a piece deliberately written in Thalberg's legato arpeggio style, and some pedal is required virtually throughout. Of course, there were differences in the pedal and damping mechanism of Liszt's pianos compared to those of today (see pp. 68–9), but none of these would affect our general conclusions here. The paucity of indications in the G minor study is all the more puzzling because the other pieces in the set, such as the C minor study, have a detailed range of pedal markings. Indeed, pedal is indicated in the C minor study even where we would not expect it. At 'Animato il tempo', the bar-by-bar pedal seems to contradict the instruction 'sempre staccato e distintamente il basso', which would be more easily achieved with no pedal at all.

The implication is that Liszt, during the period of the *Grandes études* at least, tended to indicate the use of the sustaining pedal only when the pedalling was not immediately obvious, or in order to underline a dramatic increase in volume. This would explain, for example, why the F minor study has no pedal marked at all, despite containing long passages of passionate legato melody over extended bass figuration. In the G minor study, the pedal markings at the climax might actually have been designed to prevent over-pedalling, by requesting a change at each new harmony, rather than to initiate the use of the pedal. Liszt's attitude appears to have been 'any fool can see you need pedal here'. In the transcription of Wagner's *Tannhäuser* Overture (published 1849) he made this explicit, giving no pedal indications, but writing a footnote to the effect that sensible use of the pedal was expected. This was his attitude for some of his Weimar works, although he eventually came to the view that to expect most performers to pedal his music intelligently was rather naïve.

Even during the Weimar period Liszt's approach was inconsistent. All the pieces in *Harmonies poétiques et religieuses*, published in 1853, the year of the Sonata's composition, contain detailed pedallings – except one. The Andante lagrimoso has pedal marked for only four bars – again, the climax of the piece – though all pianists would use pedal in this work at least as frequently as the others of the set. Significantly, the marked pedal here extends the bass note much further than its written value, as with the first pedalling in the Sonata, to provide a warm cushion of sound for the melody above. Liszt must have feared that otherwise this type of passage might be played in a cold and dry manner. Similar inconsistency can be seen in the six *Consolations* (1850). The famous No. 3, in D♭, is heavily pedalled, but the others not at all, though No. 6 requires nearly as much pedal, and the rest certainly some.

Of the larger Weimar piano pieces, the First Ballade (1849) has no pedalling, as might be expected in a piece published the same year as the transcription of the *Tannhäuser* Overture. The *Concert-solo* (published 1851) has frequent pedalling, perhaps partly resulting from its genesis as a conservatoire competition piece. The Second Ballade (published 1854) begins as if the pedal markings are going to be as extensive as the *Concert-solo*, but they disappear after three pages. The opposite applies to the *Scherzo and March* (1854), where pedalling suddenly puts in an appearance on the very last page of a twenty-four-page piece. The Sonata, therefore, is not particularly unusual for a work published in 1854 in its miserly pedal indications. From the late 1850s onwards Liszt, chastened by the experience of listening to ineptly pedalled performances of his music, took more care to indicate the basic requirements for each piece.

Liszt's markings for the *una corda* pedal are equally variable. Though he often indicated its use, he was cautious about writing *tre corde* cancellation instructions, perhaps assuming that any competent pianist would use his judgement as to the right moment. In the Sonata, the *una corda* and *sempre una corda* indications in the Andante Sostenuto are Liszt's own, but the *tre Corde* cancellation that we find in the New Liszt Edition at bar 363 is an editorial addition. Unquestionably the *una corda* will have to be abandoned somewhere around here, for the intense central section can hardly be given an adequate rendering with the *una corda* depressed. It seems to me that after the *fff* climax the *una corda* should be retaken, certainly for the *ppp* passage a few bars later. This is not indicated in the New Liszt Edition, despite the fact that cancellation of the original *una corda* was not specifically marked by Liszt.

Liszt was well aware that use of both pedals will vary in each separate performance according to the acoustics of the hall and the characteristics of the piano. It was this consideration that prompted him sometimes to abandon pedal markings in the first place. Accounts of Liszt's playing and teaching show that his pedalling was subtle, sophisticated and occasionally at variance with his own published indications. Both the *Liszt Pädagogium* and Sauer's edition of the Sonata give an additional *ppp una corda* at bars 162 and 164, apparently played by Liszt. Brendel, in his preface to the reprint of the *Pädagogium*, advises against making too much of this, which he thinks should be simply a nuance. Da Motta, too, could hardly have liked the effect, for he fails to mention it in his editorial notes to the Franz-Liszt-Stiftung Edition, though he was familiar with the *Pädagogium* and elsewhere prints suggestions from Liszt's pupils. Nevertheless, given the inadequacies of the instructions in the original edition of the Sonata, it is important to be aware of any additional performance information that has some claim to derive from Liszt. In this regard, I find the decision of the New Liszt Edition not to publish 'Liszt's various occasional instructions presumably made during teaching and preserved in a copy of the first edition of the Sonata now held in the Academy of Music, Budapest' misguided and unnecessarily restrictive. One might not wish to adopt every 'tradition' but one should at least be aware of them.

The evaluation of information passed down by Liszt's pupils is certainly more difficult than it might first appear. Of the Liszt pupils that edited the Sonata – Sauer, Da Motta, d'Albert, Rosenthal and Joseffy – none actually studied it with Liszt, at least as far as we can establish. Friedheim seems to have been the last person to work on the Sonata under Liszt's tutelage, and he performed it frequently during Liszt's final years. Sauer was present, as we have mentioned, during one of these performances, and perhaps relied somewhat on it for his edition. D'Albert's edition is the most copiously annotated of all, though he only took the Sonata into his repertoire ten years after Liszt's death. Indeed, his very first suggestion, that the opening notes should be played 'wie pizzicato', is contrary to the idea in the *Pädagogium* that they should sound like muffled timpani. Liszt admired d'Albert's playing tremendously, and all his annotations make cogent musical sense. They do not, however, necessarily derive from Liszt's own practice.

Undoubtedly, any edition of the Sonata by a pianist who heard Liszt play is worth careful study for that reason alone. The disagreements among these editions nevertheless demonstrate that they cannot be considered as definitive guides to a performance tradition. Sauer's edition claims Liszt's authority for the reinforcing in octaves of the bass at bars 531–2, an excellent suggestion found also in the *Pädagogium*. Whether Sauer got this idea from the *Pädagogium* itself, or from Friedheim's performance, or in some way directly from Liszt, is impossible to tell. It can thus only be evaluated by its musical suitability.

As far as questions of pedalling are concerned, Da Motta retains Liszt's scanty original pedalling as befits part of a 'complete' edition like the Franz-Liszt-Stiftung. The others add numerous pedal markings, and even alter Liszt's own pedalling at the Più mosso in the recapitulation, indicating a more frequent change of pedal than the original. The latter is no doubt partly in response to differences in twentieth century pianos, but if we look for evidence of a Liszt tradition in the additional pedallings, we come up against the obstinate fact that they are all eminently sensible, and all different. At the end of the final appearance of the Grandioso theme, for example, when the entire keyboard is set ringing with the dominant seventh of B, some pianists cut off the final F♯ chord sharply, others allow it to ring on longer (bar 710). Sauer's pedalling indicates the former, Joseffy's the latter. The two maintain their differences over the last note of the Sonata which with Sauer is similarly cut immediately off in contrast to Joseffy's more leisurely change. We are forced to the conclusion that if Liszt transmitted any specific instructions for these bars, they did not reach the ears of both Sauer or Joseffy. (As a student I once heard Jorge Bolet, an eminent interpreter of the Sonata, give a masterclass in which he berated an unfortunate victim for clipping the last note too sharply. He was convinced that it could only be played with a fairly long pedal. Would that the editions of Liszt's pupil's gave any grounds for such certitude.)

We must finally remember that the Sonata editions by d'Albert, Rosenthal, Joseffy and Sauer were not intended as 'Urtext' publications, but rather had a more didactic, interpretative purpose. It would have been regarded as unusual if great pianists such as these had put nothing of their own into their editions. At the very least they would have been expected to add extensive pedalling and to make any other changes they felt were necessary. Anything less would hardly have constituted value for money. The d'Albert edition in particular gives a remarkably detailed idea of how this master interpreted the Sonata, a work he never recorded. As such it has a very high value of its own, and well deserves reprinting. The question of how Liszt himself might have interpreted the Sonata will be considered in the next chapter.

5

Performances and pianos

Needless to say, the first performer of the Sonata was Liszt himself, who played it frequently to students and friends soon after its completion on the new Erard grand that had been recently sent as a gift from Paris. A public performance by the composer was out of the question after his much publicised renunciation of his virtuoso career. Although this renunciation was far from complete – he continued to perform for charity, and in 1855 even gave the première of his E♭ Concerto with Berlioz conducting – the Sonata's main hope of public performance lay in the hands of Liszt's pupils, several of whom took an interest in the work. This phalanx of pupils included Hans von Bülow, Karl Klindworth, William Mason, Dionys Pruckner, Hans von Bronsart, Peter Cornelius and Joachim Raff, soon to be joined by Carl Tausig and Julius Reubke. Of these, Bülow and Tausig were among the finest pianists of the century, while the keyboard talents of Bronsart, Klindworth and Mason were certainly equal to the difficulties of Liszt's larger works. (Bronsart gave the first performance of Liszt's Second Concerto a few years later.) In the early 1850s the Weimar Liszt students had formed themselves into a group they described as the 'Society of Murls', with Liszt as the 'Padischa' (President). This was analogous to Schumann's fictional 'Davidsbund' (League of David), a group dedicated to fighting for new music against reactionary or 'philistine' forces. The reasons for their choice of title are involved and amusing only for those directly concerned, in common with most 'in-jokes'. Suffice it to say that membership of the Society of Murls appeared to involve the consumption of large quantities of alcohol during meetings, a requirement made financially less onerous by the generosity of Dionys Pruckner's father, who owned a brewery. Liszt, no slacker in this regard, presided enthusiastically over the Society. According to Mason, the autograph of the Sonata originally bore the inscription 'For the Murl-library' in Liszt's hand.[1]

Mason heard Liszt perform the Sonata three times within two months. The first was on 7 May 1853 at the Altenburg, the other two in June.[2] One of the June performances saw the celebrated incident when the young Brahms

65

snoozed through the whole Sonata. Brahms was visiting Liszt to show him his early attempts at composition. Too nervous to play in front of the Master, Brahms was delighted when Liszt sight-read his *Scherzo*, op. 4, from manuscript. Mason continues the story:

A little later someone asked Liszt to play his own Sonata ... of which he was very fond. Without hesitation he sat down and began playing. As he progressed he came to a very expressive part of the Sonata, which he always imbued with extreme pathos, and in which he looked for the especial interest and sympathy of listeners. Casting a glance at Brahms, he found that the latter was dozing in his chair. Liszt continued playing to the end of the Sonata, then rose and left the room. I was in such a position that Brahms was hidden from my view, but I was aware that something unusual had taken place, and I think it was Reményi who afterwards told me what it was.[3]

Brahms had been travelling through the whole of the previous night, and the lack of sleep no doubt had something to do with his very public 'criticism' of the Sonata. Nevertheless, he continued to dislike Liszt's music, though he admired his pianism, to the end of his life – a dislike reciprocated by Liszt, who found Brahms's works, with a few exceptions, 'hygienic, but not exciting'. When Liszt sent a copy of the newly published Sonata to the Schumanns, Brahms played it over to Clara, who thought it 'frightful'. 'And now I even have to thank him for it', she whined in her diary, 'it is truly appalling'.[4] Robert Schumann, incarcerated in an asylum, never heard the work dedicated to him.

We might be forgiven for doubting Brahms's ability to give an adequate sight-reading of the Sonata, but it is unlikely that Clara Schumann would have warmed to it even with a first-rate performance. Liszt's friend and supporter Richard Pohl believed that it was necessary to hear a performance by Liszt himself to properly understand the work, and certainly its technical and musical difficulties would have rendered it a closed book to most contemporary pianists. Perhaps realising this, Liszt took upon himself the role of advocate. He had tried to keep certain pieces in practice for private performance even after his abandonment of his public career – his favourite showpiece at the beginning of the 1850s was his new arrangement of *Les patineurs* from Meyerbeer's *Le prophète*, with which he dazzled the denizens of Weimar. As the apex of his achievement as a 'serious' composer for the piano, the Sonata took centre stage when Liszt was performing to an educated musical gathering, particularly when he was visited by young musicians who might become adherents of the 'Music of the Future'. If this plan backfired with the soporific Brahms, others such as Cornelius and Pohl were moved both by the piece and by Liszt's performance, which they heard on 23 October 1854 in the Altenburg.

We can obtain some idea of these early Liszt performances from the reminiscences of those present, though we can never, alas, reproduce the performance. All of Liszt's musical gatherings were informal affairs, the sublime alternating with the jovial in a relaxed fashion. The Sonata performance heard by Cornelius was preceded by a rendition of the gentle concert study *Un sospiro,* for which Liszt apparently improvised a bravura ending. Those who know the two published, introverted conclusions to this piece might wonder how on earth a bravura ending could be made to work – probably it didn't. Liszt then gave a moving interpretation of the Sonata on his favourite Erard. This was a more remarkable achievement in that the company had just finished a long and generously alcoholic lunch (which perhaps accounts for the mutilation of *Un sospiro*). The afternoon was completed by some improvisation provided by one of the guests, the Parisian organist Lefébure-Wély.

A listener at this performance in the Altenburg would have heard the Sonata played on an instrument noticeably different from the almost ubiquitous Steinway grand of today. For diplomatic reasons, Liszt often used pianos provided by local manufacturers during his concert tours across Europe, but there can be little doubt that his favoured instrument, at least until his later years, was an Erard grand. Liszt had a long association, and personal friendship, with the Erard family. In the Altenburg his Erard piano took centre stage in the first-floor reception room, which also doubled as a music library. The Erard nestled together with the Broadwood grand that had once been Beethoven's – a visual symbol of Liszt's musical inheritance. To make the point clearer, Beethoven's death mask was also on display. Upstairs, in the 'official' music-room, two Viennese grands (a Streicher and a Bösendorfer) shared space with Mozart's spinet. By July 1854 the spinet, and indeed all other instruments, had been dwarfed by a gargantuan contraption called a piano–organ, made specially for Liszt by Alexandre et fils of Paris. This was a relative of the pedal-piano (of the type favoured by Alkan) mutated to enormous size and complexity, as if by some unfortunate dose of radiation. Its three keyboards and pedalboard operated pipes in imitation of wind instruments. Liszt had intended the piano–organ as an aid in working out orchestration, but it played some part in his musical gatherings. Those interested in musical curiosities can now see it in the Kunsthistorisches Museum in Vienna.

The piano–organ was the most grotesque outcome of Liszt's continuing interest in the development of keyboard instruments. He had written publicly as far back as the 1830s of the need for an improvement in the tonal capabilities of the piano, although he felt confident that this would soon be forthcoming. It is nevertheless a striking fact that the Sonata and most of the other masterpieces of Romantic piano music, such as Chopin's Ballades and Schumann's *Fantasy*, were written before the technological changes introduced by Steinway that effectively initiated the truly modern piano. The years between 1853, when the Sonata was completed, and 1867, when Steinways scored an overwhelming success in the Paris Exhibition with their iron-framed, over-strung grand, saw some of the most momentous changes in piano manufacture. Liszt, of course, was more aware than most of these subsequent developments. He could hardly fail to be, as many piano makers of the day insisted on sending him instruments as gifts in the hope of a valuable endorsement. Even at the time of writing (1995) Steinways are still using a letter of Liszt's from the 1880s praising their pianos, and discussing the use of the new sostenuto pedal, in their promotional literature. (He included suggestions for using the sostenuto pedal in the third *Consolation* and in his arrangement of Berlioz's *Danse des sylphes*.) A more dubious recommendation was the 'Armonipiano', for which he published a version of his arrangement of 'Salve Maria' from Verdi's *I Lombardi* in the early 1880s. By peculiar coincidence, the arrangement was published by his friend Ricordi, who also owned the patent for the 'Armonipiano'. As a preface, Liszt added the note: 'A new invention which the house of Ricordi and Finzi have just adapted to their pianos will have a happy effect here. It is an invention by which one can obtain, without moving the fingers, a tremolo like Aeolian harps ... Such a poetic sonority is impossible to achieve on pianos unequipped with the tremolo pedal, and I recommend the restrained employment of it to pianists.' Other musicians found the sonority less 'poetic', and the 'Armonipiano' was buried in the graveyard of forgotten novelties. Liszt apparently never owned one himself.

Leaving aside his monstrous piano-organ and Beethoven's Broadwood, Liszt had three grands on which to play his Sonata. They represented a fair spectrum of the pianos of the day – the Erard with its double-escapement action and penetrating tone, the Viennese instruments with their simple Prellmechanik action and more intimate sound. Unlike the modern piano, none of these instruments was over-strung, making them capable of less volume but giving them greater purity of tone. The aggressively harsh sound of some of today's pianos in the upper registers (developed in response to such passages as the end of Rachmaninov's Third Concerto) was not so obvious, lending a more delicate sound to the high treble passage work in the Liszt Sonata. The lower volume of sound produced (even on the Erard) had also to do with the design and composition of the hammers – much smaller than on a modern instrument – and of the piano frame itself. Of Liszt's pianos, only the Erard would have produced a sound anything like the thunder on bottom A now heard in the first bridge passage of the Sonata. Though Liszt may have admired increased sonority in this register, he is hardly likely to have applauded the modern overbearing treble, for pupils reported that he often played high passage work *una corda* even on his own instruments.

One other feature of Liszt's pianos that might surprise contemporary concert-goers was the weaker effect of the string dampers. The less clean damping inevitably produced a more mixed sound and required a slightly different pedal technique. To a small extent the piano itself produced its own syncopated pedalling, a technique to facilitate legato playing first described by Köhler in 1875 in his *Technische Künstler-Studien*. Finally, despite the major differences between Erard's double-escapement action and the Viennese action of the 1850s, both demanded a lighter touch and had a shallower fall of key than the usual modern piano, making virtuoso playing far less arduous. The increasing action weight of pianos during the latter half of the nineteenth and first half of the twentieth centuries caused problems for many pianists, from first-rank virtuosi downwards. Paderewski demanded modifications to lighten the action of his pianos, while Liszt's pupil Rosenthal, famous for the brilliance and speed of his fingerwork, complained that it was impossible to achieve the effects he intended on the heaviest of the new instruments.

Liszt continued to perform the Sonata privately until the early 1880s, but his pupils began to practise the Sonata soon after its completion, and it was from Karl Klindworth that Wagner first became acquainted with the piece. Wagner was in London in 1855 to conduct the Philharmonic Society concerts, and Klindworth played the Sonata to him on 5 April that year. Wagner's reaction was as effusive as Clara Schumann's had been damning:

Klindworth has just now played your great Sonata to me! – we spent the day alone together, and after dinner he had to play. Dearest Franz! Just now you were with me; the Sonata is inexpressibly beautiful, great, loveable, deep and noble – just as you are. I was profoundly moved by it, and all my London miseries were immediately forgotten.[5]

Impressed almost as much with Klindworth's playing as with Liszt's music, Wagner later asked him to arrange the vocal scores of his operas, a task that also fell to Hans von Bülow. Bülow gave the first public performance of the Sonata in Berlin on 27 January 1857, having previously studied it with Liszt. The concert, which also featured chamber music (in this case Volkmann's long-forgotten Trio in B minor), was something of a triple début, introducing Bülow, the B minor Sonata, and Carl Bechstein's first concert grand piano simultaneously to the Berlin public. According to Bülow, the audience's reaction to the Sonata was one of utter stupefaction, a response that will be familiar from the premières of some new pieces today. The newspaper critics, stupefied or not, recovered in time to pen some of the most damning reviews Liszt's music had ever elicited (a notable achievement, for it had received a few). Acquiring a minor degree of immortality by misunderstanding a major work of art, Gustav Engel sallied forth from the pages of the *Spener'schen Zeitung* (30 January 1857), determined to shoot to kill:

The second item in the concert was a Sonata by Liszt (B minor). It has the peculiarity of consisting of a single, very extended movement. Certain main themes form the basis of the whole. Among them, the first is of such a quality that one can almost discern the character of the work by it alone. The structure rests on harmonic and rhythmic effusions that have not the slightest connection with beauty. Even the first theme must be dismissed as completely inartistic. Admittedly, what we get during the development is yet worse.[6]

Lest the reader miss the point, he concluded that 'it is scarcely possible to be further away from legitimate procedures than is the case here'. Not surprisingly, a definition as to what exactly constituted 'legitimate' or 'natural' procedures (*Gesetzmässigkeit*) was nowhere to be found. For the *Nationalzeitung*, Otto Gumprecht dispersed with this degree of sophistication, and summarised the Sonata as 'an invitation to hissing and stamping of feet'.

Not all the reviews were damning. Oscar Eichberg showed some enthusiasm in the *Neue Berliner Musikzeitung*, and Bülow reported that the composer Felix Draeseke, a Liszt ally, had praised both piece and performance. Nevertheless, the hostile tone of Engel's review in particular enraged the highly strung Bülow, who immediately made the understandable mistake of writing to the *Spener'schen Zeitung* in a fury, deploring Engel's blinkered attitude. Engel, of course, replied in turn, generating the usual war of words between artist and critic. Liszt was appalled when he discovered that Bülow had taken it upon himself to reply to adverse criticism. With wisdom that was the fruit of his own ill-advised journalistic battles in Milan in 1837-8, he realised that the best response was silence, and made it a rule never to react in print to even the most vituperative remarks. In private, however, it was obvious that the frequent condemnation of what he regarded as his finest music hurt him deeply. In later years he would joke ruefully that everybody knew he was an excellent transcriber but incapable of original composition.

His disappointment at the Sonata's reception in Berlin was increased by the fact that it had diverted appreciation from Bülow's playing, which everybody agreed had been magnificent, even if they deplored his choice of repertoire. Bülow performed the Sonata three more times between 1857 and 1861. Astonishingly, it seems only to have been played once (by Saint-Saëns in an April 1880 concert in the Salle Pleyel) between 1861 and 1881, when Bülow again revived the work. Critical opinion was still harsh. It was his performance of 22 January 1881 in Vienna that drew the jibe from Hanslick mentioned in the Preface.

On first publication, the Sonata had been luckier in its review in the *Neue Zeitschrift für Musik*. Cynics might point out that the reviewer was Louis Köhler, one of Liszt's staunchest friends and supporters. Köhler discussed the Sonata's use of thematic transformation, and described how personally moved he had been by the beauty of the work. Liszt wrote a letter of thanks, especially pleased at Köhler's pointing out of the transformation of the 'hammer-blow' theme 3 into a lyrical second subject. He was also delighted with another *Neue Zeitschrift* article the following year, written by his pupil Hans von Bronsart. Bronsart could have paid Liszt no higher compliment than his claim that the Sonata was a true successor of Beethoven's last sonatas, and the inaugurator of a new era in the history of form. Unfortunately, these articles made little impression on the world at large, probably because the authors were already known as fully paid-up adherents of the 'Music of the Future'. Ironically, the view of a fine musician like Bronsart, a first-rate performer, and later the composer of a splendid Piano Concerto in F♯ minor, had, if anything, less impact than that of a non-entity like Gustav Engel.

Another Liszt student, the composer Peter Cornelius, had intended to devote a lecture to the Sonata in Vienna in 1859. This was to be part of a series of three lectures, the other two dealing with Beethoven's *Hammerklavier* Sonata and Schumann's F♯ minor Sonata. He discussed his views on the B minor Sonata with Liszt, but in the event none of the lectures took place. Cornelius, on researching his subject more deeply, realised that his knowledge was as yet too scanty to do justice to a topic as large as the piano sonata. He decided to cancel the series rather than offer the public an ill-considered and superficial discourse – a conscientiousness rare among music lecturers.

By the 1880s the Liszt student, Arthur Friedheim, had taken up the Sonata. His performances were far better received than von Bülow's, and Friedheim believed that Bülow's 'objective style of playing did not lend itself to this kind of music'.[7] In his autobiography, Friedheim proudly quoted a letter written to him by fellow Liszt student Hugo Mansfeldt:

My dear Friedheim, friend of olden days – It may interest you to hear of a remark Liszt made about you many years ago. Perhaps it was never told you. In the year 1884 the festival was held in Weimar, at that time Franz Liszt's home. I was in the audience on that occasion. The next day Emil Sauer told me that he was sitting with others near Liszt when you were playing the Sonata, and when you finished Liszt turned to those around him and said: 'That is the way I thought the composition when I wrote it'. I can conceive of no greater praise bestowed on anyone.[8]

Friedheim survived into the recording age, but, alas, his Liszt Sonata was never captured for posterity. Lina Ramann heard Friedheim's 1884 performance and was less complimentary than Liszt, describing it as 'clear in form, technically mature, but also technically cold'.[9] Friedheim later toured Europe and America playing the Sonata as part of his truly enormous repertoire. For a Carnegie Hall recital on 14 April 1891 he began with the Sonata, following it with the *Bénédiction de Dieu*, the ninth *Hungarian Rhapsody*, the two *Legends*, the *Dante* Sonata and all six *Paganini* Studies. He played two other concerts in the same week, both with equally gargantuan programmes, including Beethoven's *Waldstein* Sonata and Balakirev's *Islamey*. No wonder Friedheim's technical prowess caused Vladimir de Pachmann to exclaim 'He is not only inspired by God, he is a pupil of the devil'. Friedheim replied 'I hope that is not a comment on Franz Liszt'.[10]

Of all Liszt's students, an edition of the Sonata by von Bülow or Friedheim would have been the most valuable in transmitting Liszt's intentions. Friedheim did at least give lessons on the Liszt style to his friend Ferruccio Busoni, whose performances of the Sonata, and other major works, did much to establish them in the standard repertoire. The twentieth century witnessed performances of the Sonata by Sauer, Joseffy, Rosenthal, Bache and d'Albert, among the later Liszt students. By the 1920s it had become a familiar sight on concert programmes. Even the young Arthur Schnabel, arch-Classicist though he was, had given it a few outings, although he did not retain it long in his repertoire. Rachmaninoff played the Sonata frequently during his later concert tours. His offer to record it – and the Ballade in B minor – was unbelievably not taken up. It would surely have been a worthy counterpart to his stupendous recording of the Chopin B♭ minor Sonata. Cortot had already made a recording in the 1920s, and this was soon followed by Horowitz's famous 1932 recording. Both performances are still currently available, along with over fifty others, a number that demonstrates the Sonata's firm place in the repertoire better than anything else. If, however, we compare Cortot's recording, made seventy years ago, with a section of those made in the last ten years, we cannot fail to notice a massive change in approach covering some of the most fundamental aspects of piano playing. The same is true of recordings of other composers – the performance style of roughly 1899 to 1940, as documented on surviving recordings, is radically different from that common today. As many of the earliest recordings were made by pupils of Liszt, we might investigate their interpretative style as a guide to how Liszt expected his music to be played.

Performance practice

As might be expected of any musician, Liszt's attitude to performance changed significantly as he grew older. In 1837 he had turned his thoughts publicly to the role of the performing musician in re-creating works of art:

The poet, painter or sculptor, left to himself in his study or studio, completes the task he has set himself; and once his work is done, he has bookshops to distribute it or museums to exhibit it. There is no intermediary between himself and his judges, whereas the composer is necessarily forced to have recourse to inept or indifferent interpreters who make him suffer through interpretations that are often literal, it is true, but which are quite imperfect when it comes to presenting the work's ideas or the composer's genius.[11]

In other words, written music is only the transcription of an idea that requires a performer for realisation. The inevitably exact and lifeless notation can never delineate every aspect of that music adequately, leaving its fate substantially at the mercy of the performer's talent or understanding. The performing information contained in a score varies massively from era to era and composer to composer. A Bach Prelude may contain nothing but the notes and time signature; a piece like Grainger's *Rosenkavalier Ramble* might try to give directions that extend to the minutest details of tempo fluctuation and layered dynamics. Even the latter falls short of what is required to create living breathing music rather than a stiff mechanical sequence of notes. Most performers nowadays take it as axiomatic that their role should be limited to relaying as accurately as possible the composition as they believe the composer intended it; they should attempt to subsume their individuality in that of the composer. To do this completely is impossible, which is why one pianist's Beethoven sounds different from another's, but the aim of sympathetic accuracy is usually there.

Most nineteenth-century pianists were well aware that they had a responsibility to the composer; this was balanced by a desire to project their own individuality as well. The fact that the vast majority of Romantic pianists were composers themselves encouraged this attitude. In conservatoires nowadays musicians tend to be split into performance or composition streams (though it is still true to say that few performers have never composed, and vice versa). During the nineteenth century, all the major pianists – Liszt, Chopin, Alkan, Thalberg, Anton Rubinstein, the list goes on – were also known as composers. Some were better composers than others, it is true, but all regarded themselves as more than interpretative artists, and their compositional role often spilled over into their performances of other composers' music, in the process sometimes virtually creating a new piece. This continued well into the twentieth century. The audience at a Busoni recital of Bach's music, for example, often heard nearly as much Busoni as Bach, even when the programme did not list any 'arrangements'. Sometimes a piece became more popular in a performer's version than in the original. Around the turn of the century, Henselt's 'edition' of Weber's Rondo in E♭ was heard much more frequently than the original. So much so that most of the audience were probably unaware that it wasn't the original. Anton Rubinstein summed up the general attitude when he advised his pupils to begin by learning a piece exactly as the composer wrote it. If, after mastering it, some things still seemed capable of improvement, then the pianist should not hesitate to alter them. This approach was actually far stricter than that of some of his contemporaries, who omitted the first stage entirely. In contrast, the modern attitude is usually to deplore any attempts at the second stage – if you can't make it convincing as the composer wrote it, then don't play it at all.

During his principal years as a performer Liszt took his fair share of licence. He later said that it was chiefly his performances of Weber's *Konzertstück* that gave him a reputation as a pianist who indulged in extreme interpretative liberties, but even by 1837 he admitted the problem was more extensive than this. Like a penitent sinner he made a clean breast:

During that time [1829–37], both at public concerts and in private salons (where people never failed to observe that I had selected my pieces very badly), I often performed the works of Beethoven, Weber and Hummel, and let me confess to my shame that in order to wring bravos from the public that is always slow, in its awesome simplicity, to comprehend beautiful things, I had no qualms about changing the tempos of the pieces or the composers' intentions. In my arrogance I even went so far as to add a host of rapid runs and cadenzas, which, by securing ignorant applause for me, sent me off in the wrong direction – one that I fortunately knew enough to abandon quickly. You cannot believe, dear friend, how much I deplore those concessions to bad taste, those sacrilegious violations of the SPIRIT and the LETTER, because the most profound respect for the masterpieces of great composers has, for me, replaced the need that a young man barely out of childhood once felt for novelty and individuality. Now I no longer divorce a composition from the era in which it was written, and any claim to embellish or modernise the works of earlier periods seems just as absurd for a musician to make as it would be for an architect, for example, to place a Corinthian capital on the columns of an Egyptian temple.[12]

Written around the time of his innovative performance of Beethoven's *Hammerklavier* Sonata, which according to Berlioz was a model of textual fidelity, Liszt's contrition was no doubt heartfelt. Within a few years, however, he had a relapse of epic proportions. Numerous reviews of his concert-tours of the 1840s talk of his novel additions to Handel fugues or his tempo changes in transcriptions of Beethoven symphonies. The necessity of pleasing the crowds and earning a living indubitably accounted for a lot of this, though it must be remembered that the interpretative customs of the era permitted a large degree of freedom anyway. For Liszt's interpretative licence to be specially remarked upon, it must have been extreme. Some accounts of his later performances of the *Hammerklavier* Sonata, and von Bülow's edition, which gives an octave rewriting of a passage on the last page as Liszt's idea, show that by the 1850s he was still making small alterations to Beethoven – albeit so small that by the standards of the time they must have seemed like nothing at all.

Most of the detailed accounts of Liszt's piano teaching come from his masterclasses in the 1870s and '80s, by which time his approach had become more severe. Though he habitually played virtuoso works, and smaller character pieces, with a large degree of freedom, the major masterpieces were interpreted with a sincere fidelity that contrasted explicitly with the playing of his earlier years. Two composers in particular, Beethoven and Chopin, had become sacrosanct. He could react with an anger verging on fury at attempts to 'improve' either composer. Rosenthal told how he deplored Anton Rubinstein's alterations to the Funeral March of Chopin's B♭ minor Sonata, declaring that they turned the piece into programme music – which Chopin never wrote! (The basics of Rubinstein's interpretation can be heard in Rachmaninoff's recording.) As far as his own music was concerned, Liszt encouraged the more talented pupils – such as Siloti – to put their own ideas into his virtuoso pieces like the operatic fantasies or *Hungarian Rhapsodies*. He gave performance instructions for programmatic pieces like *St Francis Walking on the Waves* that were vastly more detailed than, and sometimes contradictory to, the published score. Often he improvised new endings which were then adopted by his pupils (see Friedheim's piano roll of *St Francis*

Walking on the Waves). What must be emphasised, however, is that he always expected the integrity of his large works – the Sonata, *Concert-solo*, *Scherzo and March*, for example – to be scrupulously observed.

Liszt would probably have been amused and delighted at Horowitz's recomposition of his second *Hungarian Rhapsody* (indeed, he admired d'Albert's cadenza, from which some of Horowitz's ideas were taken). He would, I suspect, have flown into a rage over the same pianist's alterations to the *Vallée d'Obermann*, let alone to the *Scherzo and March*, which in Horowitz's only live recorded performance is mutilated in a way that makes nonsense of the sonata structure (and also happens to sound like a massive memory lapse).

Our main sources of information on Liszt's later ideas are the *Liszt Pädagogium* – a collection of notes made by Lina Ramann on Liszt's teaching of his own works, itself based on contemporary notes taken by pianists present at Liszt's masterclasses – and the diaries of August Göllerich and Karl Lachmund (see the Bibliography). To this can be added the memoirs of his pupils such as Friedheim, Siloti, Rosenthal, Lamond, Sauer and d'Albert, and second-hand information from books like Fleischmann's *Aspects of the Liszt Tradition* (Fleishmann studied with Liszt's student, Stavenhagen). A large amount of valuable information has also been passed down orally from Liszt's pupils – Charles Rosen told me several years ago of Liszt's reaction to Rubinstein's Chopin Funeral March, a story he had heard from his teacher Rosenthal. Finally, the recordings of Liszt's pupils thankfully allow us some idea of how Liszt expected his music to *sound*. Although all Liszt's students had their own individuality, it is impossible to believe that, taken together, they cannot give us an idea of the stylistic parameters within which his music should be played.

Unfortunately, specific information on the Sonata is thin on the ground. Problems with the early recording process, which allowed only a little more than four minutes of music to be recorded continuously, meant that few long works were recorded in the early decades of the twentieth century. The Sonata was not one of them, though we do have a profusion of shorter pieces recorded by pupils of Liszt and a performance of the two concerti by Emil von Sauer, with the orchestra conducted by Felix Weingartner (another Liszt student). Of the written sources, only the *Liszt Pädagogium* contains material on the Sonata. Some of this – the 'muffled timpani' of the opening, the octave reinforcement at bars 30–1 and 531–2, the *una corda* at bars 162 and 164 – has been mentioned before, as was Liszt's association of theme 2 with Coriolan's defiance. Advice on tempo is also given. The first, $\quarternote = 72$ for the beginning of the Allegro energico (bar 8), is obviously a misprint (pervasive in the

Pädagogium) for ♩ = 72. Interestingly, when the Allegro energico direction returns at the fugue, the speed is now given as ♩ = 80, indicating a natural degree of flexibility within the basic tempi. While giving this tempo for the fugue, Liszt warns against playing it too fast. As ♩ = 80 is considerably faster than some performances today, we can see the difficulties in interpreting the frequent places in the *Pädagogium* where the tempo is described rather than given a metronome mark. A direction like 'not too slow' is rather like a cipher without a key. How slowly was the student playing to deserve this warning?

Our problems are not entirely solved by the metronome marks, however. While ♩ = 66 for the Grandioso theme seems an eminently suitable tempo, as does ♩ = 108 for the Allegro moderato of the coda, ♩ = 96 for the Andante sostenuto is ludicrously fast. We have here an example of the *Pädagogium's* other favourite type of misprint – the reversal of figures in a metronome mark. ♩ = 69 is undoubtedly what is intended here. The *Pädagogium's* last direction for the Sonata, that the final C in the bass should be held on with the pedal until the entry of the B major chord in the treble – in other words, through the treble chords of A minor and F major – is the only one I personally find difficult to accept. It does, certainly, heighten the effect of the B major chord, and would be especially easy to achieve today using the sostenuto pedal, but it also weakens the impact of the separation of registers in the cadential progression. Fleischmann gives a similar effect as a 'Liszt tradition' in a passage from the Second Ballade (albeit at a much less significant point in the work), and I see no reason to believe that the suggestion does not come from Liszt. Other pianists will, of course, make up their own mind as to its effectiveness.

In forming an overall picture of Liszt's performance style, one that can be applied to the Sonata, it is essential to study the *Pädagogium* in its entirety, along with Göllerich's diaries. There is, without question, also no substitute for a knowledge of all Liszt's music, and not just a few of the most commonly played works, for the pianist who has pretensions to be a Liszt-performer. The *Pädagogium* and associated writings show that Liszt's principal concern was always with musical characterisation and communication. His performance directions have, of course, to be interpreted in the context of the piece and its intended musical effect. To a musician unfamiliar with Liszt's style, the direction Andante con moto for *Invocation* from *Harmonies poétiques et religieuses* might seem to indicate a fairly placid albeit flowing tempo. The instruction in Göllerich's diaries is 'fast and fiery' – anything less would betray the spirit of the work. It is a pity that there is not yet an equivalent of Eigeldinger's indispensable *Chopin Pianist and Teacher* (Cambridge 1986) for Liszt, drawing together all the various sources of performance information for each piece. Such a volume would be very large, but at least it would save pianists a trawl through several different works, many of them difficult to obtain, for information on Liszt's teaching.

The following is a necessarily crude summary of some points that featured frequently in Liszt's teaching. The trouble with written information like this is that it is often only fully understood by musicians who already play in this manner. I give it, nevertheless – most of it is simply good musicianship.

(1) The music must flow in large phrases, not chopped up with over-accentuation. In lyrical works such as *Bénédiction de Dieu* this does not imply particularly fast speeds, or *alla breve* tempi, but rather manipulation of tone and articulation to produce a breathing, singing melody.

(2) The musical sense must continue through the frequent rhetorical pauses in Liszt's music. 'Don't mince it up.'

(3) *Expression should always avoid the sentimental.* Liszt was emphatic about this, and often parodied what he regarded as excessively affected playing. The still common idea of Liszt as a performer – and composer – prone to lapses of precious sentimentality could not be further from the truth. This should extend to posture – no swaying around (like Clara Schumann). Sit upright, and don't look at the keys, rather straight ahead.

(4) Piano tone is often to be imagined in orchestral terms – for example, clarinet in the central A♭ melody of *Funérailles*. According to Friedheim, even in his advanced years, when some other aspects of his technique had deteriorated, Liszt was still unrivalled in building up an orchestral-style climax on the keyboard.

(5) Figuration in melodic sections of Liszt's music should be slow, not brilliant. In upper registers he usually played filigree passage work *una corda*. He had a fondness for adding mordents and other embellishments to emphasise some parts of the melodic line.

(6) A certain flexibility of tempo is in order in most of Liszt's music.

(7) The wrong notes of a d'Albert or a Rubinstein do not matter, their inaccuracies are insignificant compared with their musical expressiveness. Splashy, insensitive playing, however, brought Liszt's wrath upon the perpetrator. In his 1941 radio broadcast on Liszt, Lamond talked about Liszt's surprising strictness and concern for musical cleanliness. Lamond's awe of Liszt's censure is still apparent in his voice after nearly sixty years.

78

Many of the above points can be illustrated in the recordings of Liszt's pupils, in particular Sauer's beautifully limpid performance of Ricordanza. Friedheim was famously unhappy with his recordings, and they are unlikely to show him at his best, yet his rigorously unsentimental, even 'modern', performance of the first movement of the *Moonlight* Sonata contrasts vividly with the Romantic soulfulness typified by Paderewski, and perhaps reflects something of Liszt's later approach to Beethoven. Liszt once parodied what he regarded as Rubinstein's wayward tempo changes in this sonata. According to Siloti, his own interpretation was understated, but unforgettable. Lest this be thought to be a criticism of Paderewski, it ought to be pointed out that his recording of *La leggierezza* is, in my opinion, one of the finest examples of Liszt playing ever recorded. Liszt's conception of rubato, according to the Lachmund diaries, was probably very different from Paderewski's – and more akin to that of Rachmaninoff – but Paderewski's 'jeu perlé' in this recording seems to sum up many of Liszt's general injunctions on beauty, lucidity and evenness of tone.

Finally, no one listening to these early recordings can fail to note some striking differences from performances of today, especially in the frequent use of various types of chordal arpeggiation and non-synchronisation between bass and treble. This is a prominent feature of Cortot's recording of the Liszt Sonata from the 1920s. Although Liszt's pupils used these techniques less pervasively than Paderewski, who represents the *ne-plus-ultra* in this regard, they were still common in their playing and were an accepted part of pianism. It is unlikely, to say the least, that this fondness for asynchronicity, with its consequent subtle web of rubato and layered-voicings, arose first with this generation of pianists. Brahms, apparently, spread almost every chord in his own playing. Liszt, I believe, must have played in a similar fashion to his pupils in this respect. Were the apocryphal Liszt cylinder recording ever to turn up, it might give the critics who describe this style of playing as merely late Romantic excess a surprise. The imaginative Romantic attitude to arpeggiation and rubato is as much a part of the music's performance style as the appropriate treatment of ornamentation is in Mozart. It is to be hoped that the transfer of so many historic recordings on to CD will promote a re-examination of this aspect of Romantic pianism.

The compositional legacy

Liszt's Sonata does not only live on in performance, but also in the works of other composers. By 1855, only one year after its publication, the Sonata had spawned progeny in the Sonata in B♭, op. 1, of Rudolf Viole (1825–67), a former Liszt composition student. The obscurity of this work is such that I have been unable to obtain a copy for study, but according to Bülow's review in the *Neue Zeitschrift für Musik*, 95 (1856), it was modelled on Liszt's Sonata, and indeed utilised a theme given by Liszt to Viole in the course of his studies. Newman quotes part of Bülow's review in *The Sonata Since Beethoven*; I am relieved to note that he was unable to find a copy of Viole's Sonata either.[13] The one thing we can say for sure from all this is that Viole's Sonata sank without trace soon after its publication, which is not true of the Sonata in B♭ minor by another of Liszt's students, Julius Reubke (1834–58), who died of consumption soon after its completion, in the traditionally Romantic manner. Reubke's *Sonata for Organ*, based on Psalm 94, is frequently performed; the Piano Sonata in B♭ minor has a less secure place in the repertoire, but is nevertheless a splendid work.

Reubke's Piano Sonata is obviously fashioned after Liszt's in form and style, although it shows certain original features that demonstrate burgeoning powers of independent musical invention. The outline is notably indebted to Liszt: a one-movement form with a central Andante maestoso and 'scherzo' (Allegro agitato) recapitulation. Reubke's opening section is far more of a self-contained first movement than Liszt's, sporting its own recapitulation in the tonic key of both the main themes (bar 220 ff), although a possible cut is indicated that would eliminate the return of one of these. Ironically, this appears to be far more appropriate to Newman's analysis of Liszt's Sonata than the Liszt Sonata itself. Reubke's 'scherzo', too, though not so described, is at least in 6/8 and more obviously a conventional scherzo than Liszt's, the second subject of Reubke's Sonata forming the basis of a trio section at bar 487 ff. This scherzo performs the 'double function' of being a recognisably independent entity and also the greater part of the recapitulation. The coda completes the recapitulation with a return of the second subject, which as the trio of the scherzo remained in the secondary key of F♯ major, for a tonic apotheosis. Reubke's Sonata is a truly remarkable example of a young composer immediately grasping the significance of his master's formal and harmonic innovations and proceeding to develop them along his own lines. His control over the language of the 'Music of the Future' is all the more striking in that his few compositions before the piano and organ sonatas show little awareness of the musical avant garde. Some aspects of Reubke's Sonata perhaps reveal the influence of Schubert's *Wanderer* Fantasy, in particular the greater extent of the scherzo section compared with Liszt's Sonata, and the use of the second subject as the basis of a trio. The scherzo's function as tonic recapitulation, however, differs from Schubert's *Wanderer* Fantasy, where the tonic return is marked by the fugal opening of the final section. That Reubke intended his Sonata to be a tribute to Liszt's teaching is confirmed both by the dedication and by the quote of part of theme 2 from Liszt's Sonata at bars 42–3. There can be little doubt that a great talent was extinguished with Reubke's early death. When in 1885 Reubke's Sonata was performed in a Weimar masterclass by the American pianist William Dayas, Liszt was visibly moved.

Another Liszt acolyte, Felix Draeseke (1835–1914), produced a *Sonata quasi Fantasia,* op. 6, heavily influenced by Liszt's Sonata in its cyclical construction, but definitely leaning more towards the *Fantasy* than the Sonata. The piece was published in 1870 with a dedication to Bülow. Liszt spoke highly of Draeseke's work, but this was, I hope, in recognition of his attempt at formal originality rather than in admiration of the quality of the resulting music. In his powers of invention Draeseke was notably inferior to Reubke, and his op. 6 is now of little more than historical interest.

This is far from the case with the final Liszt Sonata epigone, the Sonata in F minor, op. 27 (1908), by Sergei Liapunov (1859–1924). Liapunov was a pupil of Balakirev, with whom he shared a passionate love of Liszt's music. He had earlier been a student of Karl Klindworth, to whom he dedicated his own Sonata, perhaps in recognition of Klindworth's advocacy of the Liszt prototype. Liapunov's Sonata is modelled even more closely on Liszt's Sonata in B minor than is Reubke's. Not only is the formal outline copied (again, the 6/8 scherzo is far more obviously a scherzo than Liszt's), but even specific features like the building up of a dominant chord *fff* in octaves under a tremolo before the introspective coda (bar 571). The keyboard style relates exactly to Liszt's, with certain figurations recalling not just the Sonata but also the *Bénédiction de Dieu* (bar 338 ff) and the *Scherzo and March* (bar 382 ff). Liapunov deserves credit, however, for at least one difference: the sharing of the first-subject group between an energetic and then a lyrical theme (bars 1 ff and 52 ff). The latter sounds as if it ought to be the second subject, despite the fact that it is firmly in F minor. The ensuing transition and presentation of a new cantabile theme, in D major (bar 108 ff), disabuses us of our initial impression and ingeniously expands the exposition to a length and thematic complexity adequate to match the remainder of the expanded form. Liapunov probably found the germ of this idea in Liszt's *Grand Concert-solo*. Liapunov's Sonata is not a work of the very first rank, but it is melodically strong and carries off its debt to Liszt with some panache. The keyboard writing is skilful and well contrasted; it justly rewards any pianist willing to tackle it for, despite some very tricky passages in the scherzo, it generally sounds more difficult than it actually is. Of course, the influence of Liszt's Sonata extends more widely than the genre of the piano sonata alone – Schoenberg's First Chamber Symphony (1906) is certainly a close relative – but the Liapunov is the last of the sonatas that might be called copies, rather than distant successors.

Both Reubke and Liapunov regarded a scherzo section as an essential feature of the Liszt Sonata formal type, and we find a similar three-movement-in-one plan in Eugen d'Albert's Second Piano Concerto, undoubtedly influenced by the Lisztian model. D'Albert's own Piano Sonata in F♯ minor, however, takes its inspiration from Beethoven (particularly the *Hammerklavier* Sonata) rather than Liszt. The Sonatas by Reubke and Liapunov are fine works deserving of far more frequent performance; at present they are heard but rarely. No doubt one of the reasons for this is the ubiquity of Liszt's Sonata itself, which now has such a firm place in the repertoire that its successors are in permanent eclipse, a situation that Liszt could hardly have foreseen after its initial contemptuous reception. Happily, the reputation of Liszt's Sonata seems to have paralleled that of the dramatic figures whose strivings he so delighted in setting to music – from *Lamento* to *Trionfo*.

Notes

Preface

1 Hanslick, *Concerte, Componisten und Virtuosen*, p. 316.

Introduction

1 The sketch of the Sonata's first two motifs, from Weimar sketchbook N2, is reproduced in Winklhofer, *Liszt's Sonata*, p. 171. The Andante sostenuto sketch was supposedly contained in a sketchbook belonging to the Chopin specialist Arthur Hedley (Winklhofer, *ibid.*, p. 93). Since his death in 1969, its whereabouts have been unknown.
2 La Mara, ed., *Letters of Franz Liszt*, I, pp. 186–7.
3 Quoted from Chantavoine, *Franz Liszt: Pages Romantiques*, pp. 134–5.
4 La Mara, ed. *Briefwechsel zwischen Franz Liszt und Carl Alexander*, p. 8; letter of October 1846.
5 It is obvious from Liszt's correspondence that Rotondi, who is given as the author of *Sardanapale* in most works on Liszt, supplied a libretto for an opera called *Ricardo alla terza Crociato*, but had nothing to do with *Sardanapale*. The author of the scenario (in French) for *Sardanapale*, now in the Weimar Archive, was Jean-Pierre Félicien Mallefille (1813–68), a French novelist and playwright. Mallefille's play *Les Deux veuves* was to be the basis of Smetana's opera *The Two Widows*. Mallefille's *Sardanapale* scenario reached Liszt only after he had already commissioned an Italian libretto from an un-named friend of Princess Belgiojoso, and it was this libretto that he began to set to music. The Mallefille scenario is simply yet another red herring.
6 La Mara; ed., *Letters of Franz Liszt*, II, p. 33, letter to Dr Franz Brendel, 8 Nov., 1862.

Forms and formulae

1 La Mara, ed., *Letters of Franz Liszt*, I, p. 151; letter to Wilhelm von Lenz, 2 Dec 1852.
2 Marie von Bülow, ed., *Hans von Bülow: Briefe und Schriften*, III, p. 50.
3 Robert Schumann, *Music and Musicians*, pp. 259–60.
4 *Ibid.*, p. 274.
5 La Mara, ed., *Letters of Franz Liszt*, I, p. 273; letter to Louis Köhler, 9 July 1856.
6 *Ibid.*, p. 296; letter to Alexander Ritter, 4 Dec. 1856.
7 *Ibid.*, p. 274; letter to Louis Köhler, 9 July 1856.
8 *Ibid.*, pp. 151–2; letter to Wilhelm von Lenz, 2 Dec. 1852.
9 Liszt, *Gesammelte Schriften*, II, p. 106.
10 Schumann, Music and Musicians, II, pp. 102–3.
11 An interesting discussion of this and other features of the Romantic sonata style can be found in Charles Rosen, *Sonata Forms*, pp. 365–403. For a detailed consideration of Schumann's *Fantasy* see Marston, *Schumann: Fantasie, Op. 17*.
12 Friedrich Schnapp, 'Verschollene Kompositionen Franz Liszts', p. 22. Schnapp reproduces the autograph of the F minor Sonata between pages 128 and 129. His separate listing of a fourth,

C minor, sonata (p. 126) seems to me to be erroneous. This work is probably identical with one of the two other sonatas of 1825.

13 La Mara, ed., *Franz Liszts Briefe an Seine Mutter*, p. 30.

14 See R. Larry Todd, 'Liszt, Fantasy and Fugue for Organ on "Ad nos, ad salutarem undam"', *19th Century Music*, 4 (1981), pp. 250–61, for a perceptive analysis of this piece.

Understanding the Sonata in B Minor

1 Winklhofer, *Liszt's Sonata*, p. 115.
2 Newman, *The Sonata*, p. 373.
3 See Walker, *Franz Liszt: The Weimar Years*, p. 151, fn 45. Walker gives no source for this information, which he presumably obtained from surviving Dohnányi students.
4 Raabe, *Franz Liszt: Leben und Schaffen*, II, pp. 59–62.
5 Szász, 'Liszt's Symbols for the Divine and Diabolical'.
6 Merrick, *Revolution and Religion in the Music of Liszt*, pp. 283–95.
7 Bertrand Ott, 'An Interpretation of Liszt's Sonata in B minor'.
8 Ramann, *Liszt Pädagogium*, V, p. 3.
9 Newman, *The Sonata*, p. 375.
10 My references to Longyear's analysis are taken from his summary in *Nineteenth-Century Romanticism in Music*, pp. 162–5. This condenses his more extensive discussion in *Music Review*, 34 (1973), pp. 198–209.
11 Ramann, *Liszt Pädagogium*, V, p. 3.
12 La Mara, ed., *Letters of Franz Liszt*, I, p. 157; letter to Louis Köhler, 8 June 1854.
13 Brendel, *Music Sounded Out*, p. 177.
14 Ramann, *Liszt Pädagogium*, V, p. 3. See also Sauer's Peters edition of the Sonata.

Text and texture

1 La Mara, ed., *Letters of Franz Liszt*, p. 330; letter of March 26th, 1857 to Edward Liszt, 26 March 1857.

Performances and pianos

1 Mason, *Memories of a Musical Life*, p. 159. The manuscript seen by Mason was possibly a copy of the one now extant, which of course bears a dedication to Schumann.
2 *Ibid.*, pp. 123–7.
3 *Ibid.*, p. 127.
4 Berthold Litzman, *Clara Schumann: Ein Künstlerleben*, II, p. 317; diary entry of 25 May 1854.
5 Erich Kloss, ed., *Briefwechsel zwischen Wagner und Liszt*, II, p. 65; letter of 5 April 1855.
6 Bülow, *Briefe und Schriften*, IV, pp. 65–6.
7 Friedheim, *Life and Liszt*, p. 181.
8 *Ibid.*, p. 141.
9 Lina Ramann, *Lisztiana*, ed. Arthur Seidl (Mainz, 1983), p. 240.
10 Friedheim, *Life and Liszt*, p. 3.
11 Suttoni, *Artist's Journey*, p. 31.
12 *Ibid.*, pp. 17–18.
13 Newman, *The Sonata*, pp. 404–6.

Select bibliography

Brendel, Alfred: *Music Sounded Out* (London, 1990)

Bülow, Marie von (ed.): *Hans von Bülow: Briefe und Schriften*, 8 vols. (Leipzig, 1895–1908)

Chantavoine, Jean: *Franz Liszt: Pages romantiques* (Paris, 1912)

Egert, Paul: Die Klaviersonate in H-moll von Franz Liszt, *Die Musik* 28/2 (1936), pp. 673-82

Fleischmann, Tilly: *Aspects of the Liszt Tradition* (Cork, 1986)

Friedheim, Arthur: *Life and Liszt* (New York, 1961/*R* 1986)

Göllerich, August: *Franz Liszt* (Berlin, 1908)

Hanslick, Eduard: *Concerte, Componisten und Virtuosen der letzten fünfzehn Jahre*, 1870–85 (Berlin, 1886)

Hudson, Richard: *Stolen Time: A History of Tempo Rubato* (Oxford, 1994)

Jerger, Wilhelm (ed.): *Franz Liszts Klavierunterricht von 1884–1886 dargestellt an den Tagebuchaufzeichnungen von August Göllerich* (Regensburg, 1975)

Kloss, Erich (ed.): *Briefwechsel zwischen Wagner und Liszt* (Leipzig, 1910)

Lachmund, Karl: *Living with Liszt*, ed. Alan Walker (Stuyvesant, NY, 1994)

Liszt, Franz: *Gesammelte Schriften*, ed. L. Ramann, 6 vols. (Leipzig, 1880–83)

Litzman, Berthold: *Clara Schumann: Ein Künstlerleben* (Leipzig, 1906)

Longyear, Rey: 'Liszt's B minor Sonata: Precedents for a Structural Analysis', *The Music Review*, 34 (1973), pp. 198–209

    Nineteenth-Century Romanticism in Music (Englewood Cliffs, NJ, 1973)

    'The Text of Liszt's B minor Sonata', *The Musical Quarterly*, 60 (1974), pp. 435–50

La Mara (ed.): *Franz Liszts Briefe*, 8 vols. (Leipzig, 1893-1902)

    Letters of Franz Liszt trans. Constance Bache, 2 vols. (London, 1894)

    Briefwechsel zwischen Franz Liszt, und Carl Alexander (Leipzig, 1909)

    Franz Liszt: Briefe an seine Mutter (Leipzig, 1918)

Marston, Nicholas: *Schumann: Fantasie, op. 17* (Cambridge, 1992)

Mason, William: *Memories of a Musical Life* (New York, 1901)

Merrick, Paul: *Revolution and Religion in the Music of Liszt* (Cambridge, 1987)

Newman, William: *The Sonata since Beethoven* (New York, 1972)

Ott, Bertrand: 'An Interpretation of Liszt's Sonata in B minor', trans. Sida Roberts and P. Vaugelle, *Journal of the American Liszt Society*, 10 (1981), pp. 30–8, and 11 (1982), pp. 40–1

Raabe, Peter: *Franz Liszt: Leben und Schaffen*, 2 vols. (Tutzing, 1968)

Ramann, Lina: *Franz Liszt als Künstler und Mensch*, 3 vols. (Leipzig, 1880–94) *Liszt Pädagogium*, 5 vols. (*R* Wiesbaden, 1986)

Rosen, Charles: *Sonata Forms* (New York, 1988)

Saffle, Michael: *Franz Liszt: A Guide to Research* (New York, 1991) 'Liszt's Sonata in B minor: Another Look at the 'Double Function' Question', *Journal of the American Liszt Society*, 11 (1982), pp. 28–39

Schnapp, Friedrich: 'Verschollene Kompositionen Franz Liszts', in *Von Deutscher Tonkunst: Festschrift zu Peter Raabe's 70 Geburtstag*, ed. Morgenroth (Leipzig, 1942)

Schumann, Robert: *Music and Musicians*, ed. Ritter, vol. 2 (London, 1880)

Suttoni, Charles: *Franz Liszt: An Artist's Journey. Lettres d'un bachelier es musique 1835-1841* (Chicago, 1989)

Szász, Tibor: 'Liszt's Symbols for the Divine and Diabolical: their Revelation of a Programme in the B minor Sonata', *Journal of the American Liszt Society*, 15 (1984), pp. 39–95

Walker, Alan: *Franz Liszt*, vol. I *The Virtuoso Years* (rev. edn London, 1988); vol. II: *The Weimar Years* (London, 1989)

Watson, Derek: *Liszt* (rev. edn London, 1990)

Winklhofer, Sharon: *Liszt's Sonata in B minor: A Study of Autograph Sources and Documents* (Ann Arbor, 1980)

Index

Index